MERRY LUNDOW
Fourth edition revised by Howard Clarke

Discovering
Country Walks in
North London

D1013491

SHIRE PUBLICATIONS LTD

To my wife

Maps by Merry Lundow
Photographs by Cadbury Lamb
Cover design by Ron Shaddock
This edition revised by Howard Clarke

British Library Cataloguing in Publication Data. A catalogue record for this book is available from the British Library.

Published in 1995 by Shire Publications Ltd, Cromwell House, Church Street, Princes Risborough, Buckinghamshire HP27 9AA, UK. Copyright © 1978 and 1995 by the executors of the late Merry Lundow. First published 1978, second edition 1981, third edition 1988, fourth edition 1995. Number 240 in the Discovering series. ISBN 0 7478 0265 3.

Printed in Great Britain by CIT Printing Services, Press Buildings, Merlins Bridge, Haverfordwest, Dyfed SA61 1XF.

Contents

4

Foreword

London has never quite relinquished the countryside which nurtured her; and perhaps the proudest boast of this proud old city, the Llyn-din – 'river place' – of the Celts, is that she contains within her boundaries today remnants of her own ancient countryside greater in their variety than those of any other city in the world. Some of them, like the central Royal Parks, with their fine groves of trees and great lakes, and Hampstead Heath – Macaulay's 'swarthy moor' – lie close to the heart of the capital; others, like the birch-clad commons of Stanmore and Harrow Weald and the rolling farmlands of Barnet and Enfield, link up with the rural areas beyond the city's borders to form part of the London green belt, portions of the Home Counties that were lopped off and incorporated in the new Greater London in 1965.

In this book of walks, their length modest enough to prove ideal for family outings no less than for solitary rambles, some of my favourite country walks in my own north London are described. Many of them are circular, bringing motorists back to their parked cars; but, where they are not, starting and finishing points are usually connected with each other by direct bus or train service.

Walking is one of the most natural, as well as health-giving, of pleasures, and few tips are needed for those who may be about to follow a book of walks for the first time. I would, however, mention footwear, a pair of comfortable old shoes always being my first choice—leather ones in winter so that mud, inevitably encountered here and there on the short days, may wash off harmlessly and easily under the tap at home. Dogs should be kept on leads when crossing fields where animals are grazing; and the Countryside Code should be honoured at all times, e.g. gates left fastened, single file observed along field paths, care taken not to leave litter or cause damage through fire, and wild flowers left unpicked so as to provide pleasure for those who follow.

Finally, whether you try just one walk in this book or – if you are energetic enough – end up by following them all, perhaps in something like the order in which they have been written so that the gradual unfolding of London's ancient rural heritage may prove a constant source of interest and delight, there is one thing of which I am absolutely certain: you will never walk alone. For beauty will accompany you always... in the bluebells of woods in spring, the sweet-scented dog rose of winding summer lanes, the joyous song of the skylark welcoming you to the open fields and meadows at all seasons of the year.

Hampstead Garden Suburb

Publisher's note on the fourth edition

The late Merry Lundow published these walks in 1978 and revised them three years later. They have been further revised subsequently, and although this latest edition has been rewalked and checked by Howard Clarke, the routes are substantially the same as Merry Lundow's, varied only by minor footpath diversions. Despite a further decade and a half of development and road-building, the scenery on these walks still unfolds to surprise and delight the eye, a tribute to Merry Lundow's skill in planning the original routes, and a fitting memorial to a man whose book has brought so much pleasure to those who follow his footsteps.

The view to Buckingham Palace from St James's Park.

1. Gardens of the Queen

From Charing Cross (Embankment station) to High Street Kensington station: 4^1/$_2$ miles.

Many hold the Royal Parks to be the glory of London, and certainly there is nothing finer than the country walk that may be taken through the great chain of Royal Parks which stretches for two and a half almost uninterrupted miles from Westminster to Kensington. St James's Park, Green Park, Hyde Park and Kensington Gardens – each link is a lovingly tended garden of the Queen, its freedom long ago granted to the people of London by one of the Queen's royal forebears. Here is a variation of this popular 'through' route which combines the grandeur of Whitehall and the old-world charm of Shepherd Market village with paths that run delightfully amid trees and flowers, by lakes where pelicans swim and yachtsmen sail, and where London indeed seems far away. They end at the doors of Kensington Palace, where we may visit the State Apartments and see the room in which Queen Victoria, as a girl of eighteen, heard the news of her accession.

Leave Embankment station by the Villiers Street exit and turn left under Embankment Place, modern headquarters of Coopers & Lybrand. Keep forward over a crossing road and through Victoria Embankment Gardens opposite. Turn right in the first road you come to (Horse Guards Avenue) and, with the Ministry of Defence left and the War Office right, follow it to Whitehall. Cross to the Horse Guards opposite, noting through the archway the Guards Memorial across the parade ground, our route into St James's Park.

First, however, turn left down Whitehall – past the Scottish Office and Privy Council and Cabinet Offices – and just before the Cenotaph look into Downing Street through the iron gates. The building on your left houses the Foreign and Commonwealth Office. The Prime Minister's house, Number 10, and that of the Chancellor of the Exchequer, Number 11, are on the right. Now retrace your steps to Horse Guards and turn left through gates between the mounted guards and forward into St James's Park – once Henry VIII's deer park – and past the Guards Memorial.

Keep the lake just to your left, looking out for the pelicans, but, before passing the bridge, stand in the middle of it to admire two famous London views. Some hundred yards beyond the bridge branch off right to cross – with great care on weekdays – The Mall, the royal ceremonial driveway from Buckingham Palace (seen left).

Continue opposite to view Stable Yard Road through iron gates. Clarence House, right, London home of Queen Elizabeth the Queen Mother, was built by Nash for William IV when Duke of Clarence, the Royal Standard flying when royalty is in residence.

Retrace your steps back to the Mall, and turn right towards Buckingham Palace. In 100 yards turn right on to an enclosed path (Queen's Walk) with railings right. In 100 yards, with a security gate to Lancaster House on your right, turn left into Green Park, an addition to St James's Park made by Charles II. Queen's Walk was named after Queen Caroline, wife of George II, whose private promenade it was. Strike squarely into the park along the path starting just left of the tall lamp-post; but soon, just beyond a junction of many paths, turn squarely right on the Broad Walk, just before the Canadian war memorial with maple leaves embossed on the water sculpture, and follow this avenue of plane trees all the way to Piccadilly. Cross the road, turn left past Lord Palmerston's house, then go right along White Horse Street to Shepherd Market, the old village-heart of Mayfair, with its restaurants, antique shops and art galleries.

Follow Shepherd Market round left along a paved courtyard, turning left at Trebeck Street, where a wall-plaque commemorates the fair that gave the district its name, and right along Shepherd Street. Go forward beneath the buildings, and forward still up Stanhope Row and Pitt's Head Mews beside the Hilton Hotel to Park Lane. Cross this by the pedestrian subway, at the end of which turn right up steps to enter Hyde Park – the ancient Manor of Hyde – by a small gate.

Follow the forward path to a junction of several paths. Take the half-left (i.e. second leftward) path, keeping straight on along it, over roads. Among flower beds now, and with the broad sandy ribbon of Rotten Row appearing 50 yards ahead, turn right on a path running between sloping lawns. Bear right on a crossing path, with the wooded hollow known as The Dell (where the river Westbourne flows) on your left; then ease left around a café, with the Serpentine now on your left.

Keep on along the delightful lakeside path but, on drawing level with a tree-clad island, turn right up a lamp-posted road past a pillar box left, to the picturesque police station. (The Royal Parks have their own police force.) Bend sharp left with the road (the pretty house, right, is that of the Park Superintendent) but in 150 yards take a short rightward road to nursery gates. Resume leftward beside railings, soon passing the Hudson Memorial Garden, with its Epstein sculpture, and now maintain your forward direction to cross a horse-ride and road, and turn left along the latter.

Follow this road, keeping right past the elegant Magazine, once

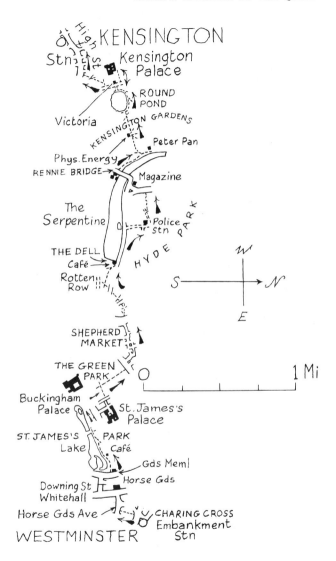

a military arsenal. Cross the graceful Rennie bridge, then turn immediately right into Kensington Gardens, formerly the grounds of Kensington Palace.

Unless diverting left to visit the Serpentine Gallery, take the rightmost path and follow it on beside the lake to the Peter Pan statue, beloved of generations of London children. Retrace your steps for 100 yards, fork right on a lesser path, then immediately branch off right again and follow to the equestrian statue of Physical Energy.

Resume your forward direction along the metalled path leading towards Kensington Palace, now seen clearly across the park in the direction in which the horse is facing. When this ends at a crossing path keep forward over grass to the Round Pond, following the path rightward around it to reach, on the far side, the statue of Victoria, clad in the night attire she was wearing when news of her accession reached her. The sculptor was the Queen's daughter, Princess Louise.

Unless omitting the State Apartments turn right on the Broad Walk; in a few yards a signpost points left to the Apartments by way of the beautiful Sunken Garden – a replica of that laid out by Queen Anne – with its fine pleached lime tunnel. Returning to Victoria's statue, continue past it for 100 yards, turn right on a broad path, then at once go left on a path running diagonally across parkland. A fine vista of Wren's splendid palace façade opens up behind you as you follow on out to Kensington High Street. Go right along this famous London thoroughfare, past St Mary Abbots Church, to the station.

TRANSPORT
Embankment station: Underground (Circle, District, Bakerloo and Northern Lines). *High Street Kensington*: Underground (Circle and District Lines). *Motorists:* direct service High Street Kensington to Embankment by Underground (Circle Line).

2. Along the canal

From King's Cross station to Baker Street station: 4 miles.

The architect John Nash worked for the day when a great canal would link the London docks with the inland port of Paddington, adding a new dimension to the London scene with horse-drawn barges and narrowboats gliding through an urban landscape. With the building of the Regent's Canal Nash's aim was achieved. Then came the railways and the roads, luring away the teeming traffic of the canal until its waters fell silent, disturbed only by the cries of waterfowl. Today, with cruise-boats and other leisure craft plying its length, Nash's old dream is being revived, and walkers may roam along the quiet backwaters of St Pancras and Camden Town, following the towpath through a fascinating world of canalside buildings, bridges and locks little altered since the industrial revolution. We pass Camden Lock and in a sudden burst of greenery find ourselves amid the terraces of Regent's Park Zoo. Deer and antelope abound; storks eye us, one-legged, as we pass.

Leave King's Cross station by the exit at the front of the main-line station, turn left in Euston Road and keep ahead along Pentonville Road. Turn left along Caledonian Road. Fork right with it, and in a quarter of a mile – at the Thornhill Arms – turn squarely right and keep on along Wynford Road. Turn left along Muriel Street, cross the Regent's Canal bridge, and enter a gate on the left half way along Muriel Street to gain the canal where it emerges from the three-quarter mile long Islington Tunnel. Follow the towpath now, soon passing Battlebridge Basin. Away to your left are King's Cross and St Pancras stations and the gasholders of what was once the Imperial Gas Light Company, for many years dependent upon the canal for its supplies of coal.

Soon after rounding a bend we come to St Pancras Lock, with its lock-keeper's cottage but no lock-keeper. (Before the Second World War there were two.) Just beyond this is the St Pancras Yacht Basin, where the railway wagons tipped their loads of coal for further transportation by barge. Now come a railway bridge and then the Oblique Bridge, a restored road bridge (with vertical railings) surviving from the days of the notorious Agar Town, which occupied the land on your right. A canalside settlement of several hundred ill-kempt, often waterlogged shanties, Agar Town was campaigned against by Charles Dickens and eventually re-placed by the railway goods depot which now stands on the site.

Beyond the St Pancras Way road bridge (with the Constitution inn standing beside it) the canal winds through Camden Town beneath a succession of road bridges. Note the grooves worn in the iron bridge protectors caused by the ropes used to pull the boats by horse. Grooves can also be seen on the handrails of the footbridges that are crossed on this walk. Two more locks follow – Kentish Town and Hawley – then, just beyond the next bridge, a third lock – Hampstead Road – is reached, the middle of three horse-changing stages between Limehouse and Paddington. The mileage signs here read ' Liverpool 302 miles, Birmingham 146 miles'. At this point the towpath along the right-hand side of the canal comes to a temporary end. Cross over by the lock and then recross by the pedestrian bridge which takes you to where the footpath resumes. The towpath may always be regained by way of Dingwall's Timber Wharf, now occupied by the workshop village known as Camden Lock, built around a cruise-boat terminal and incorporating restaurants, craft shops and a market.

Resuming along the towpath, just beyond a road bridge the 'pirate castle' of the Pirate Club for children, founded by Lord St David, rears its battlements; before and after the next bridge (Stevenson's railway bridge) are a pair of horse-slips, ramps built into the towpath to assist horses which had plunged into the canal on being startled by passing trains.

Now the canal sweeps on, under the ancient Grafton Bridge (note the plaque) and past St Mark's church, to enter the Cumberland

'Blow-up Bridge' on the Regent's Canal.

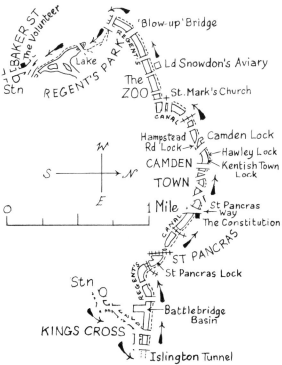

Basin, now a mooring place for private craft but once the junction with an arm of the canal serving the Cumberland Market near Euston station. Passing down the long wooded cutting of Regent's Park we obtain a canal's-eye view of the Zoo, including Lord Snowdon's towering aviary, right, just beyond a new footbridge. The second bridge beyond this is the Macclesfield road bridge, known as 'Blow-up Bridge' since the explosion of 1874 when a train of barges laden with gunpowder collided with the bridge and blew up, killing its crew and causing such widespread damage that the resulting claims hastened the financial decline of the Regent's Canal Company. Note the tow-rope abrasions on both sides of the Doric columns, indicating that in the reconstruction of the bridge they were re-erected in reverse.

Leave the canal at the next bridge and turn over it into Regent's Park, keeping forward over a road and along a wide footpath. Two successive right forks bring you to a bridge over the boating lake;

13

cross this and turn left beside the lake, with the mosque and Nash's handsome terraces away right. Just before the next bridge turn squarely right to a road. Ahead of you are the park gates: go through these and cross the main road, twist right and left and in 25 yards turn left down Baker Street. On the opposite side of the road, just past the Volunteer inn, is 221b Baker Street, the 'address' of Sherlock Holmes. A plaque on the wall of the Abbey National building marks the spot. Continue down Baker Street to the station.

TRANSPORT

King's Cross station: British Rail; Underground (Hammersmith & City, Metropolitan, Circle, Northern, Piccadilly and Victoria Lines). *Baker Street station:* Underground (Hammersmith & City, Metropolitan, Circle, Bakerloo and Jubilee Lines). *Motorists:* direct service Baker Street station to King's Cross station by Underground (Hammersmith & City, Metropolitan or Circle Lines).

Keats House, Hampstead.

3. Walking with Keats

Full round from Hampstead station: 4¹/₂ miles. Shorter round from Hampstead Heath station, omitting Hampstead village: 4 miles.

Hampstead Heath has always been dear to the hearts of north Londoners and to none more so than that of the poet Keats, who lived at Hampstead and delighted in the untamed beauty of the heath and the old-world charm of the villages and hamlets clustered about its edges. In this first of three heathland rambles we visit the house in which the poet spent the happiest period of his life and walk in the garden in which the immortal *Ode to a Nightingale* was written. Millfield Lane, still a country lane, was the scene of the celebrated encounter between Keats and Coleridge, while on the lofty brow of the heath at Hampstead the poet, 'long in city pent', found it

> '… sweet to look into the fair
> And open face of heaven…'

Most walkers will wish to view the paintings at Kenwood House, the great house on the heath remodelled for the first Earl of Mansfield by Robert Adam.

On leaving Hampstead Underground station go left down the High Street and in a quarter of a mile – just before the police station – turn left along Downshire Hill. Fork right at the church; just beyond the library, right, is Keats House.

To reach Keats House from Hampstead Heath station cross the main road and turn up Heath Hurst Road opposite. Follow this round to Keats Grove, where turn right. After visiting the house all walkers keep on to the end of Keats Grove, cross the green opposite and turn left on the path running along its right edge. Follow it up on to the heath and round, right, making your own way now past two Hampstead Ponds, and taking second right to pass between the second and third ponds. Keep forward along the main (metalled) path, and, when this soon forks, keep right, passing into the open and on up Parliament Hill, named after the Parliamentary forces who, during the Civil War, planted cannon on it for the defence of London. The hill commands fine views, with the heights of Highgate seen to your left.

Follow the main path down the hill until, at a junction of paths, a minor left fork carries you away downhill to a crossing path near the corner of the first of the Highgate Ponds. Follow this left, past two ponds, to a path junction, where bear half-right to follow the main path on beside a third pond. At the end of this go right

15

between ponds. Fork left beside the railings, turn left on a lane (Millfield Lane) and follow it as it winds prettily along the wooded edge of the heath, continues forward as a path and, after picking up left-hand railings again, follows them forward to Kenwood House.

Turn left through gates and keep forward along the broad terrace: to your right is the cafeteria, once the coach house and still housing the old family coach. At the far end of the house turn right through a leafy arch to reach the main drive at the front of the house, taking a narrow metalled path past a post displaying 'May peace prevail on earth' in English and Japanese, and on reaching the far end of the lawn descend left beside it to a crossing path. Turn left, then, in a few yards, right on a broad cross-track. Do not follow the main track rightward through a hedge-gap, but keep left instead downhill beside a right hedge with a Henry Moore sculpture on your left; and when this path turns away right through a low fence bear left instead over grass – still beside a right fence alongside a pond to the right – until a path is reached, on which turn left. When the ornamental bridge comes into view – just around a bend in the path – leave the path to go right over grass. Keep by the hedge, then left by the water's edge, a delightful spot familiar to those who attend the lakeside concerts staged here during the summer. The charming Georgian 'bridge' towards which we now turn right on a metalled crossing path is just a beautiful sham,

Kenwood House, Hampstead.

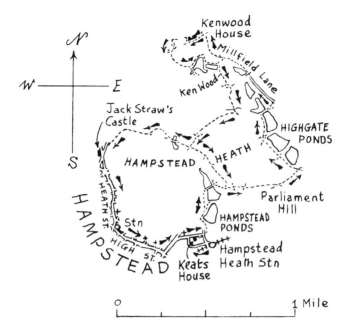

having been erected by the first Earl of Mansfield for effect only.

Beyond the 'bridge' keep left uphill and go straight on along the left edge of the woods to a corner, and straight on again through the open along a metalled path.

Cross a spring by a culvert. Now the path turns away left, at which point turn back very sharply right – almost full about – on a narrow track running beneath overhanging trees. Keep forward along this fine track, disregarding any cross-tracks, and when in a quarter of a mile it dips slightly to reach a junction of many paths twist left and right to resume your forward direction along a broad avenue of tall lime trees. Soon you reach a wide crossing path: for the full round back to Hampstead station turn right and pass on to the next paragraph; for the shorter round turn left and keep straight on along the beautiful path, ignoring a left fork later, until finally it becomes enclosed and swings round right. Retrace your outward steps now between the Hampstead Ponds and on round left to follow the main track past two ponds, and round left to follow the left edge of the green back to Hampstead Heath station.

Resuming on the full round, a viaduct soon carries you high

17

above a pond (full of lily pads in summer), the main track sweeping on now for nearly half a mile, climbing all the way to reach the brow of the heath at Spaniards Road, some 400 feet above sea level. Jack Straw's Castle will be on your right as you turn left in the road past the Whitestone Pond (where early morning riders still water their horses) and drop down fashionable Heath Street to Hampstead station.

TRANSPORT

Hampstead station: Underground (Northern Line). *Hampstead Heath station* (South End Green), British Rail (North London Line).

Fenton House, Hampstead.

4. Dick Turpin's inn

Full walk from Childs Hill (Castle inn) to Temple Fortune (Royal Oak inn): 6 miles. Short circuit from Hampstead station: 4 miles.

A walk to the Spaniards, the country inn on the edge of Hampstead Heath, always makes a popular outing on a fine weekend morning. The story goes that the ancient hostelry was a favourite haunt of Dick Turpin, the highwayman stabling his horse (the Black Bess of legend) in the old toll-house opposite. True or false, the heath was certainly notorious for the depredations of Turpin's kind during that lawless era! Here is a very beautiful Spaniards walk, winding along wooded heathland ways and affording en route a glimpse of some of the quaint streets and alleyways of old Hampstead village, where poets and painters lived and worked in England's golden age. It ends in Hampstead's lovely Garden Suburb, itself a paradise of parks and woods and picturesque cottages and houses.

Both Childs Hill and Temple Fortune, our starting and finishing points, lie within a minute or two's bus journey of Golders Green Underground station (Northern Line). Starting at the Castle, Childs Hill, turn up Hermitage Lane beside the inn. Keep to the left-hand footpath and when the road bends right at the top of the hill keep forward behind a shrubbery. Cross a road and go straight on along a bridleway on Hampstead Heath. Soon you pass the Leg of Mutton Pond, with the gates of Golders Hill Park opposite.

In another 250 yards – when exactly level with a second set of gates – take the track half-right uphill through the birchwoods. On the crest of the hill lie a large uprooted birch tree and, to its right, a fence. With the latter on your right, go forward on the path uphill and follow it to the gates of the The Hill garden. Once the grounds of Lord Leverhulme's house, this is well worth visiting, its Pergola Walk, reached by steps beyond the pond and entwined in summer with wistaria and roses, being particularly fine. Resume now along the main track to a hospital drive, and at posts opposite take a path running downhill under an arch.

Here we are joined by those doing the short circuit, and all walkers now follow this very ancient path around left beside a left wall. When the wall finally ends keep forward on a broad, almost parallel track coming in over your right shoulder, and later turn right on a wide cross-track with stone guttering. Just before reaching a road turn sharp left, almost 180 degrees, on a sandy track which passes between two clumps of silver birch trees: ignore any cross-tracks, following it out, by way of a final hummock, to a road. A narrow track – sometimes rather faint – now climbs the hill opposite to reach the edge of Hampstead village at Windmill Hill.

Follow this forward downhill and over roads, then quickly turn left along Admiral's Walk. Sir George Gilbert Scott lived at Admiral's House, the 'Romantic House at Hampstead' painted by Constable and owned in the eighteenth century by Admiral Barton, whose habit it was to fire a cannon from the roof at times of rejoicing! John Galsworthy lived next door at Grove Lodge, 'birthplace' of many of the later generation of Forsytes. At the end of the Walk turn right along Hampstead Grove, passing George du Maurier's house, left, and – opposite this – Fenton House, a William and Mary house, now owned by the National Trust, with remarkable contents and a delightful walled garden open to the public.

At the foot of the grove stands Romney's house, left, while just beyond this a narrow street, Holly Mount, leads to the Holly Bush tavern, dating back in part to 1625 and charming in its simple authenticity. From here the short circuit to Hampstead station may be completed by continuing along Holly Mount for a few more yards, descending steps on the left and turning right in Heath Street. But for the full walk ascend the railed footpath which begins opposite the entrance to Holly Mount, turn right on a crossing path, and at once go left along Mount Vernon.

Those setting out from Hampstead station on the short circuit may reach Mount Vernon by following the left-hand footpath up Holly Hill and bearing left at the top. All walkers now proceed along the quaint little street, turning left at posts down Holly Walk. The Catholic church, left, was founded by French emigrés at the time of the Napoleonic Wars. At the foot of the hill stands the parish church of St John: its exquisite gilded interior should be seen, entry usually being possible by the side door if not by the front porch. From the latter a path descends to the foot of the churchyard and the tomb of John Constable.

Leave the churchyard by the main gates. In the corner of the cemetery, left, the grave of Hugh Gaitskell adjoins those of famous stage folk. At the far end of elegant Church Row turn left in Heath Street, immediately right along Oriel Place, left in High Street, then immediately right along Flask Walk. Keep on along its left-hand (raised) footpath, bearing right later past the baths and so forward along Well Walk. Constable painted at Number 40 during the summer months. Opposite is a pump, all that remains of the chalybeate wells that once made Hampstead a fashionable spa, visitors taking their morning promenade in the shade of the tall lime trees lining the raised footpath.

Keep forward over the main road and on along the track oppo-

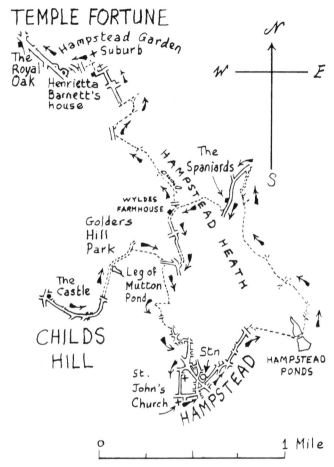

TEMPLE FORTUNE

Hampstead Garden + Suburb

The Royal Oak

Henrietta Barnett's house

The Spaniards

HAMPSTEAD HEATH

WYLDES FARMHOUSE

Golders Hill Park

The Castle

Leg of Mutton Pond

CHILDS HILL

St. John's Church

Stn

HAMPSTEAD

HAMPSTEAD PONDS

0   1 Mile

site, and at the end of the block of flats turn right on a crossing path. In a few yards fork left, the little path now meandering over the open heath to the Hampstead Ponds. Bear slightly left between two ponds, and just beyond them leave the metalled path for the middle track of three seen leading off left. Go over two crossing paths, but at a third (quickly reached) turn left uphill, with the heights of Highgate now appearing right. Keep left through trees shortly – just above a playing field – and on along the left-hand of two

21

*The well head in Well
Walk, Hampstead.*

forward tracks, ignor-
ing cross-tracks and
side tracks.

On reaching the iron
railings of Ken Wood
follow a broad ride
forward over a rise
(with the railings
right) and past two
iron gates, ignoring
the gravel path lead-
ing to Kenwood
House, taking instead
the main leftward
path, which soon runs
out on to open
heathland. At a fork in
a quarter of a mile
keep left, but, with the path now curving right, leave it to keep left
over grass towards a field gate. Pass through the swing-gate beside
it and carry straight on past cottages to a road, where go left uphill
to the Spaniards Inn.

Just beyond the inn go half-right through posts over a small
green, cross a drive, fork right immediately and follow the little
path downhill through woods, with houses right. Just before a road,
swing left on to a track running parallel to it through the trees. On
reaching houses, for the full walk ignore the remainder of this
paragraph and the whole of the next; for the short circuit to
Hampstead station keep straight on, passing Wyldes Farmhouse,
with its associations with Linnell, Dickens and Sir Raymond Unwin.
The track becomes a lane, swinging round left to crossroads at
Hampstead North End; here keep forward, passing in a few yards
Pitt House, right, the gateposts and drive being still there although
two modern villas now stand on the site of the house in which the
elder Pitt once lived.

Keep forward for 50 yards to steps, right, leading through a gap in the original garden wall of the house. Two alternative routes now present themselves: one being to follow the road – it soon becomes a track – uphill and round, right, to the main road; the other – for those who do not mind going slightly off the beaten track to discover a historic relic – being to turn through the gap along a grassy, uphill path, and follow it round left to find, under a tall beech tree, a solitary archway of Pitt's demesne still surviving. Beyond the arch the track runs on along the right edge of the wood to the road. In any event cross the road and go up the drive opposite (Inverforth Close), signposted to The Hill garden. At posts in 80 yards, unless diverting along the rightward track to visit the garden, described near the beginning of this ramble, fork left on a path running downhill under an arch and refer back to the same paragraph for further directions.

To resume the full walk from the houses mentioned earlier, descend right to cross the road and follow the forward path to a drinking fountain and on downhill, a belt of oak trees on your left. Ahead may be seen the tall spire of the parish church of St Jude, Hampstead Garden Suburb, and, to its right, the clock-tower of Henrietta Barnett School and Institute, all designed by Sir Edwin Lutyens. Pass outbuildings, cross a sandy bridlepath, and keep straight on along the forward path to a road. Turn right in the road, then quickly right again on another path. When a wooden plank bridge leads off right, ease left towards the great wall of the Suburb and in a few yards go right up steps, along a paved path and up a road to the doors of St Jude's church.

Unless visiting the church – its interior, beautified by Walter Starmer's wall and ceiling paintings, should not be missed – turn left beside the church wall to the end of a cul-de-sac, with Dame Henrietta Barnett's house (marked by a plaque) facing you. Turn right between posts and follow the path through the beautiful Central Square, the heart of the Suburb, with the domed Free Church (another Lutyens building) ahead of you and the Henrietta Barnett School and Institute across the square, right. At the Henrietta Barnett memorial you should descend left between tennis courts to a road. Turn right and, in a few yards, left on an enclosed path which runs down to a road and on again, opposite, to a drive. Turn right in this and right in the road to the Royal Oak inn and bus stops at Temple Fortune.

TRANSPORT

Hampstead station: Underground (Northern Line). *Motorists:* direct service Temple Fortune (Royal Oak inn) to Childs Hill (Castle inn) by bus.

5. Over the heath to Highgate

Full round from Golders Green station: 6½ miles. Shorter round from Highgate Village (South Grove), omitting Golders Green: 5½ miles.

Another village beloved of the poets was Highgate, Hampstead's twin sister across the heath, its heights dominated by the church in which Samuel Taylor Coleridge lies buried. Opium-addicted and penurious, the 'most spacious intellect that has yet existed among men' lived nearby on the charity of the kindly Gillmans; and on this most beautiful of heathland walks we shall see the house in The Grove where the poet of *Kubla Khan* and *The Ancient Mariner* spent his last years. Another Highgate poet was Andrew Marvell and, although his cottage with its 'garden of my own' adjoining the grounds of the Earl of Lauderdale's house is no more, Lauderdale House itself, where Charles II would install Nell Gwynne whenever the Earl was away in Scotland, still remains. The gardens in which the lovers strolled must have been very beautiful then; yet we ourselves may wander there today amid comparable splendour, for they now form part of Waterlow Park, one of two exquisitely lovely parks which we shall be seeing on this walk, the other being Golders Hill.

Many walkers will wish to visit the ancient Flask inn, the scene of much revelry in olden days. And there is also the Gate House inn, standing on the site of the 'high gate' erected at the top of Highgate Hill ('Turn again, Whittington') to gather tolls from travellers along the Bishop of London's road, thereby giving the village its name. Through this gate one day in 1554 rode the young future queen, Elizabeth, a forlorn figure at that moment for she was a captive of her ambitious sister, Mary, then on the throne of England. Elizabeth was being brought from Ashridge to the Tower of London, there to languish for many long weeks as Mary's prisoner.

I have added to the walk one optional extra which many visitors associate indelibly with the village: the tomb of Karl Marx in Highgate's leafy cemetery.

Leave Golders Green station by the main exit, make for the Hippodrome and turn down West Heath Drive opposite. At the end of this turn left, then immediately right to enter Golders Hill Park shortly by a wooden gate, left. Go right to follow the right edge of this beautiful park all the way to a crossing path; here turn right and pass out of the park through iron gates.

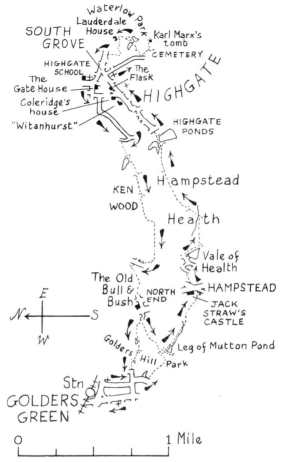

Keeping the Leg of Mutton Pond on your right, go round it to its far end and follow a spring forward through a valley. Keep the stream on your right until an open space (with a road beyond) is seen away right, then, with the stream on your left, follow the right edge of the woodland forward beside the open space, and make for the flagstaff at the Whitestone Pond along any path you choose.

Unless halting for refreshment at Jack Straw's Castle, left, cross the main road and take the path beginning at steps opposite the war

25

memorial. Observe in the distance ahead of you Highgate church, with the mansion of Witanhurst to its left. Quickly fork right, then take the left-hand of two forward paths which divide and descend to the Vale of Health, the lakeside hamlet where Keats came to thank Leigh Hunt for publishing his first poem. Cross the road and turn right along an alleyway. South Villa, left, and, as we shall see shortly, North Villa lay claim to having been built on the site of Leigh Hunt's little cottage, and certainly his spirit cannot be far away from this delightful spot.

At a small square turn left past Tagore's house and left again to a road junction. Before turning right past D. H. Lawrence's house keep forward a yard or two more to note North Villa. Resume the walk now to reach a crossing drive, where turn right. At the far end of the lake turn left on a clear track, and left again later on a broad avenue of lime trees. In a while this ancient trackway emerges into the open to run straight over the heath, with Highgate appearing directly ahead. Pass between two Highgate Ponds, fork right up-hill, and keep ahead up Merton Lane. At the end of this climb left, past Holly Terrace, a white-walled terrace of eighteenth-century houses, and, behind its surrounding wall, left, the mansion of Witanhurst, built in 1913 by the soap tycoon Sir Arthur Crosfield. At the top of the hill lies Highgate village.

Turn left immediately, mount the steps across the entrance drive to Witanhurst, and go forward to Number 3 The Grove, where Coleridge lodged with the Gillmans for eleven years. Retrace your steps now and cross the road to the nineteenth-century St Michael's church.

Coleridge is buried beneath the centre aisle, and the stone bears his own epitaph. There are also memorial tablets to the poet and the Gillmans on the north wall.

Leaving the church, go sharply right in the road. Over to your left is the Flask inn. In beautiful Pond Square, site of the old village pond, stands Moreton House, right, Coleridge's first Highgate home, the two top left-hand windows of the old house marking his room. Turn right down Swain's Lane for a quarter of a mile to a white lodge, left: the way now lies left through the iron gates of Waterlow Park just beyond it, but those who do not mind a small diversion may first visit the tomb of Karl Marx in Highgate Cemetery by passing through the next set of gates, following the drive and forking left with it to a sharp bend.

Resume now through Waterlow Park, left at a triangular island, then quickly forking right downhill to pass, over a stone bridge, between two lakes. Fork right again and at an aviary turn left uphill to a wide crossing path. Go right on this, with the domed Roman Catholic church of St Joseph soon appearing ahead, and turn left

Waterlow Park, Highgate, and St Joseph's church.

shortly up successive flights of steps to Lauderdale House.

Go left around the garden, passing the charming floral sundial with its dedication by Andrew Marvell, whose cottage stood only a few yards from here. Turn left through the gap in the wall and right beside the spacious lawn sloping down to the lake. Pass the statue of Sir Sydney Waterlow, the last owner of Lauderdale House, with its bronze umbrella; and a few yards beyond this look left through the trees for a fine view of St Paul's Cathedral. Turn right on a crossing path by another pretty lake to reach a road (Highgate Hill). Turn left up the High Street.

Pass the entrance to South Grove, left, with its attendant bus stops for those starting or finishing the walk here. A little further up the High Street is Highgate School, founded in the sixteenth century by Sir Roger Cholmeley, a Lord Chief Justice of England. The first of the red-brick buildings is the school chapel, where Coleridge was first buried, and opposite this is the Gate House inn.

Just beyond the inn turn left down Hampstead Lane, left again in The Grove and, in a few yards, right down Fitzroy Park, a pretty little private road open to walkers. When, at the foot of allotments, the road bends sharply left, turn off right along a little road lined with cottages and at the end of these turn, through iron gates, squarely left on a narrow fieldside track. Keep forward over a lane and climb the metalled path to the entrance to Ken Wood, right.

Turn in here, fork left uphill, and resume direction just inside the left edge of the beautiful wood. Ignore the first right turn in 200 yards, take the second, and follow it into the heart of the wood,

27

keeping left all the way. Just before a low tree-stump of giant girth, where iron railings begin on your right, turn right out of the wood through wooden gateposts and along a track. At the second set of gates in the iron railings, left, turn through them; then go right – keeping the railings on your right – through trees at first, then along the right edge of a playing field, with the railings now replaced by a wooden fence.

On reaching a corner turn right and follow the fence-side track as it runs over a hospital drive and on again to reach a road. Here you should cross the road and follow the little track down the slope opposite. Turn right, pass above a hollow, and in a few yards gain a clear crossing track dotted with benches. Turn left along this beautiful woodland track. Later it runs above marshes and, with a wooden fence now ahead, bears half-right downhill, then half-left past the corner of the fence to a road at Hampstead North End. Keep forward in this to cross the main road at the Old Bull and Bush, the tavern of the music-hall song and a favourite haunt in their day of Reynolds, Gainsborough and the actor David Garrick.

Turn up Sandy Road opposite, winding with it past pretty houses and bearing left at the end on a sandy bridleway. In a few yards go right through an iron gate into Golders Hill Park, those finishing at Golders Green station taking the forward path winding downhill past a café, and passing on to the next paragraph. Unless diverting for refreshments or exploring the beautiful park further, those doing the shorter round should keep to the left edge of the park, with its fine north-westerly views, the green-roofed medical research institute at Mill Hill being visible in clear weather 5 miles away. Pass on your left iron park gates to the Leg of Mutton Pond, from which point further progress may be made by referring back to the beginning of this ramble.

Continuing to Golders Green, keep left of a duck pond and, at its far end, keep on again downhill, with a shrubbery on your right, to a crossing path. Go right on this, forking left immediately to pick up the right edge of the park and follow it out to a road. Go forward down this to the main road, where turn right for the station.

TRANSPORT

Golders Green station: Underground (Northern Line). *Highgate Village (South Grove):* buses.

6. Garrick's manor-house

Full round from Brent Bridge or Brent Cross station: 6 or 6¼ miles. Shorter walk from Hendon (Church End) to Brent Bridge. 4½ miles.

It is said that David Garrick hardly occupied Hendon Hall, the mansion he built on becoming Lord of the Manor of Hendon in 1756, preferring to reside at Hampton or at the Adelphi. Be that as it may, a stroll out to the beautiful manor-house, now a hotel on the edge of the London Green Belt, makes a splendid ramble, always full of interest and with many fine moments, our route taking in Sunny Hill, with its lovely old church and marvellous panoramic view, and winding Ashley Lane, its rustic charm never failing to delight visitors to this part of old Hendon. Ashley Lane is also full of history, for it was along this ancient bridlepath that the great Cardinal Wolsey, dismissed after long years of service to his king, came riding with his servants on his last journey to York.

If starting from Brent Bridge (saving a quarter of a mile on the full round) proceed – with the bridge on your right – along the right-hand side of the North Circular Road. Just before the railway viaduct turn right up a side road. If starting from Brent Cross station leave by the Heathfield Gardens exit, turn downhill to the North Circular Road and cross to the turning opposite (Shirehall Gardens) by means of the footbridge. On crossing the river Brent note the house, left, once the home of music-hall comedian Little Tich. Ahead lies Hendon Park: take the path running along the foot of the railway embankment, fork right in 100 yards, and, at a drinking fountain on the other side of the park, ease slightly left to follow the right edge of the park all the way out to a road.

Keep forward along the alleyway opposite, crossing a road shortly (Sydney Grove). Ignore all cul-de-sacs, cross another road in a quarter of a mile and, 100 yards beyond this, branch off left down another fenced path to a main road (The Burroughs), where turn right. Pass Hendon's handsome town hall, library, fire station and Middlesex University and turn left along Church End.

Bear left with the road: before you stands the parish church, while beyond the Greyhound inn is the seventeenth-century Church Farm House, Hendon's oldest dwelling house and well worth a visit if time permits. The thirteenth-century church still retains its Norman font, while a stone let into the floor left of the high altar marks the grave of the founder of Singapore, Sir Stamford Raffles.

With the church on your left follow the winding path through the churchyard to a lane. Turn left and go out on to Sunny Hill. Keep forward by the right edge of the parkland, with its magnificent views to west and north: beyond the railway line in the near distance – watch for a passing train to mark its path – are the Grahame Park housing estate and the arch-roofed Royal Air Force Museum, both built on the site of Hendon aerodrome, birthplace of British aviation and famous for the pre-war air displays which were watched by thousands thronging the slopes of Sunny Hill.

In a while the path runs downhill and sweeps on, over crossing paths, to the Great North Way. Go under this road, mount steps opposite, and turn right on a path running along the right edge of fields. You are now in Copthall Fields, once the great park of a private mansion, and the green-roofed building on the northern skyline is the National Institute for Medical Research at Mill Hill. Soon Copthall Sports Stadium comes into view, left.

Church Farm House, Hendon.

30

Turn right on an access road but, just beyond a club-house, go left through a car park and continue along the right edge of a playing field beside back-garden fencing. A short enclosed path carries you on into Archfield allotments. Go left along the main footpath and at the far end of the allotments keep forward through a swing-gate and on beside a right hedge with Hendon Golf Course sometimes visible through it. Later the path veers away from the hedge, passes through a swing-gate at the far end of the fields and runs hard right – above a dismantled railway line – to steps leading up to a road by a bridge.

Go right in the road to crossroads, where turn right down Ashley Walk. When this bends left, keep forward between posts along Ashley Lane, with Wolsey riding northwards towards you. The lovely path leads first along the edge, then down the centre, of the golf course. When, later, it becomes a road, keep forward still, and at the Great North Way turn left to traffic lights. To visit Hendon Hall turn right up Parson Street – past the back of the hotel to its arched entrance in Ashley Lane. The front of the manor house can be viewed through the arch. The courtyard has two obelisks: one dedicated to David Garrick, the other to William Shakespeare, whom Garrick greatly admired. Now retrace your steps to the traffic lights.

Continue as before along the left-hand side of the Great North Way, but in a few yards descend steps on your left and resume direction along a sunken footpath, with bungalow gardens left. At a side road go left – ignoring a left bend in a few yards – through a traffic barricade to a bridge over the river Brent. Turn right along the wooded riverside path, go over a road (or under it by subway) and resume beside the river opposite. At the confluence with the Mutton Brook in a quarter of a mile keep forward over an iron-railed bridge to a road (Bridge Lane). Go left in this, but in a few yards turn right through gates into Brent Park.

Fork right immediately on a path which bends left to run between the river and the lake, in which fine reflections may sometimes be observed. At the end of the lake a stone bridge leads to a path junction. Here turn sharply right, passing children's swings and roundabout, and, with the river soon reappearing right, follow the path out to the road. Turn right for the road junction at Brent Bridge.

If continuing to Brent Cross station keep forward along the left-hand side of the North Circular Road. Just short of the railway viaduct turn left up Heathfield Gardens. The station approach path is on your right.

TRANSPORT

Brent Cross station: Underground (Northern Line). *Hendon (Church End)*: buses. *Motorists:* direct service Brent Bridge to Hendon (Church End) by bus.

7. Among the Quakers

Round trip from Mill Hill Broadway station: 4¹/₂ miles.

When the Quakers fled to Mill Hill from the religious persecutions of Charles II's Cavaliers they built a meeting house, which still stands today in the lovely old village. George Fox, the first of the Quakers, came there to worship; another was the botanist Peter Collinson, to whose Mill Hill garden came many of England's nobility in search of exotic plants for their estates. Collinson befriended many of the fellow Dissenters who came to his door, among them the American Quaker Benjamin Franklin, whom he introduced to the Royal Society and encouraged in his studies of electricity. What more appropriate, then, that a Protestant Dissenters' grammar school should one day open its doors in Collinson's old house on The Ridgeway! Today it bears the proud name of Mill Hill School; and on this delightful walk we shall view its present fine buildings from the best possible vantage point – the beautiful school grounds which were once Peter Collinson's garden.

On leaving Mill Hill Broadway station turn right along Station Road, then right along Woodland Way to a crossing road. From gateposts opposite a path leads through Mill Hill Park. Just beyond a tunnel take a rightward path zigzagging across the park to back-garden fencing. Just short of the fencing descend towards square, flat-roofed houses, to a side road. Go left in this, right in another road (Parkside) to a crossing road (Copthall Drive), then right, then shortly left at a road junction into Bunns Lane. Then go left up Page Street, the old Roman road to Mill Hill.

At the T junction with Wise Lane turn left, but at once go right on a path with wooden railway sleeper steps and ascend through woodland into Arrandene fields. Keep to the forward path, ignoring all side tracks and cross-tracks as it plunges across scrubland and picks up a left hedge. Keep by the hedge (crossing a sandy bridle-track shortly) to reach a stile in a corner.

Continue forward now along a terraced footpath, with the playing fields of Mill Hill School on both sides. When the path peters out keep straight on over grass (passing right of trees) to pick up an enclosed path running right of Ridgeway House, one of the school's seven houses. Go right in a road, then squarely left on a signposted public footpath starting just beyond Collinson House (named after Peter Collinson).

Follow the path downhill through the school grounds, ignoring side tracks and cross-tracks, with Harrow Hill church discernible, left, on its five-mile-distant height, and across the playing fields, right, the Ionic portico of School House, built in 1825 by Sir William Tite. Later St Joseph's missionary college appears on an eminence ahead of you, its campanile topped by a gilded statue of the saint. Finally the path drops to a road, where turn right uphill. Near the top of the hill, and marked by a plaque, is the house occupied by Sir James Murray when, as a master at Mill Hill School, he began his great work on the *Oxford Dictionary*.

At the Three Hammers inn turn right along The Ridgeway, Mill Hill's fine old village street, with its fine views northward over the Totteridge valley. Pass on your left St Paul's church, founded by the slave-trade abolitionist William Wilberforce, who lived at nearby Highwood Hill, and later the charming house occupied by the headmaster of Mill Hill School. Opposite this is the front of School House, with its Corinthian Gate of Honour standing before it, while a few yards further on a plaque on a wall marks the site of Peter Collinson's house.

At a fork by a red public telephone box note, left, the white weatherboarded Rosebank – the original Quaker meeting house, now a farm – but fork right down the little High Street and keep right down the steep slope of Milespit Hill. In a quarter of a mile, and with the bottom of the hill now in sight, turn in right through a gate by the fence of Tomlin (Number 83) and in 50 yards through a small gap in the hedge, left, leaving the horse track, re-enter

School House and playing fields, Mill Hill.

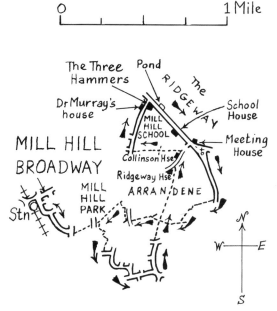

Arrandene fields.

Keep straight ahead through this field to cross a ditch by a culvert and pass through a gap in the hedge ahead. Turn left on a hedge-side track which leads to a gap on your left in 50 yards. Pass through here and climb straight up the centre of the hill by a grassy track. On the crest of the hill turn right to follow a wide cross-track through hedge gaps, and continue absolutely straight on again to join a clear track sweeping in from the right. Keep left along this as it drops to a roadside swing-gate.

Go right in the road, at once picking up a path running parallel to it just inside the edge of Mill Hill Park. Zigzag with it to a main crossing path. Go left on this, with the domed buildings of London University Observatory soon coming into view through the trees, right. Ahead lies the tunnel of your outward journey, through which your steps may be retraced to Mill Hill Broadway station.

TRANSPORT

Mill Hill Broadway station: British Rail Thameslink line from London.

8. A cardinal's village

Full round from Mill Hill East station: 6¹/4 miles. Shorter round from Totteridge (Orange Tree inn), omitting Mill Hill East: 4 miles.

Beyond Mill Hill the Totteridge valley farmlands slope down to the winding Folley Brook and up again to the old-world village of Totteridge straggling along its ridge, still the pretty country retreat for Londoners that it always was, and, it is to be hoped, always will be, for it is one of the 'picture villages' of north London's countryside. It was here, in 1808, that Cardinal Manning was born, and although his actual birthplace, Copped Hall, has long since been demolished, those who come to Totteridge must inevitably pass by the spot where it stood, for it lies just opposite the lovely church with the weatherboarded bell-turret that has been a landmark to travellers for almost three centuries. Here is a walk, full of beauty in itself, that includes several of the beauty spots for which Totteridge is famous, not least the pretty pond at Laurel Farm, where we obtain our first glimpse of the village to come, and another, with its ducks and its geese, at the sign of the Orange Tree inn.

On leaving Mill Hill East station turn right under the railway bridge and follow the main road to a roundabout. Keep left along Dollis Road. On a sharp right bend – just beyond the thirteen-arch Northern Line viaduct – a metalled path signposted 'Dollis Valley Green Walk' strikes left over the Dollis Brook and into woodland. Follow it – with the brook right – along the edge of Finchley Golf Course, with a glimpse to be had of the nineteenth-century mansion of Nether Court, now the course club-house.

When a red-brick bridge carries a lane across your path continue opposite on a rough track running between the brook, right, and a pond. Beyond this the forward path becomes metalled again, but, at a second wooden footbridge, leave the stream for a rough track rising leftward across the golf course. In a while the track reaches the golf club drive and runs out to a road. Turn right and, on a right bend in a quarter of a mile, go left along Partingdale Lane. Bend sharply right with it past the entrance to the housing estate of Inglis Barracks but, when it bends left again, leave it to continue forward along an enclosed track – Burtonhole Lane.

When in a while this enclosed track or lane bends sharply left, climb over a gateside stile, right, signposted to Totteridge. Follow the track by fencing, then between fields and over the Folley Brook

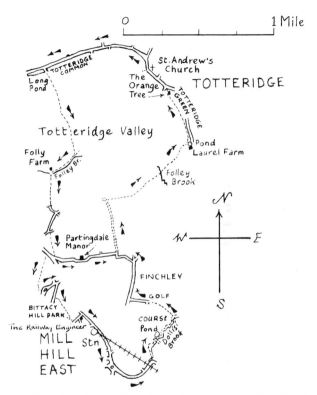

to a gateside stile at Laurel Farm. This gives on to an enclosed path which leads out to a duck pond at Totteridge Green – a delightful spot. Strike squarely left now on a clear track which skirts the left edge of the green beside houses and cottages. Finally it passes the back of the Orange Tree inn (with its lovely pond before it) to emerge at a main road which is really the village street of Totteridge.

With the Orange Tree on your left, turn along the main road, using the footpath, right, to reach the next landmark, the parish church of St Andrew, with its yew, 27 feet in girth and reputed to be a thousand years old, standing before its front porch. Cardinal Manning's birthplace (Copped Hall) stood on the site of The Darlands opposite.

Continue on, passing the war memorial on your right, following the major road for about a mile to Long Pond. At Long Pond turn

The Orange Tree and pond, Totteridge.

left on a drive which starts just before it, and immediately go over a signposted stile and follow an enclosed path (with fields to your right) down the long slope of the Totteridge valley. Expansive views now open up before you, the southern skyline being dominated by Mill Hill Ridgeway's green-roofed medical research institute, and that to the south-east by the four-mile-distant television mast of Alexandra Palace.

The lovely track finally ends at the Folley Brook, where turn right on a brookside path and follow it to the gates of Folly Farm. From here a lane leads left past a cricket ground and nurseries to a crossroads, where go right, take the first left turn (Eleanor Crescent), and immediately go right along a woodland track. Follow this out to a road junction at Mill Hill Ridgeway, where 'full-rounders' returning to Mill Hill East station should turn right in the main road and ignore the next paragraph.

For the shorter round go left down Partingdale Lane, soon passing Partingdale Manor, left, a lovely old house to which local tradition ascribes a priest's hole (hiding place) dating back to the religious persecutions of Restoration times. When the lane bends sharply right, turn left instead on an enclosed track (Burtonhole Lane) and refer to directions given earlier.

To continue the full round leave the main road in 100 yards for an enclosed metalled path on your left which drops downhill and commands fine south-westerly views. At a road a pathway leads left to another road: turn left uphill, take the first right turn (Bittacy Rise) and at a flat-roofed house in 200 yards turn left on an alleyway into a park. Follow the path straight downhill and at the bottom bear left to a road. A left turn, and a right turn in the main road, will lead to Mill Hill East station.

TRANSPORT
Mill Hill East station: Underground (Northern Line).

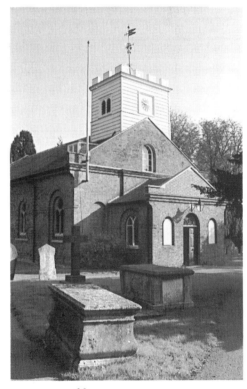

St Andrew's church, Totteridge.

9. Lord Lytton's bell

Full round from High Barnet station: 7¹/₂ miles. Shorter walk from Totteridge & Whetstone station to High Barnet station: 6 miles.

There are many fine and rewarding footpaths leading across the broad green Totteridge valley, yet none with more charm than the one which begins beside the Folley Brook and flies like an arrow over the open fields and up the side of what was once the great park of Copped Hall, to emerge, after a final twist and turn, at Totteridge church in the heart of the beautiful village. Copped Hall, mentioned in connection with Cardinal Manning in our last walk, was at one time owned by Lord Lytton, and I never follow this route without visualising the great novelist sitting in his boat in the middle of Darlands Lake dictating *The Last of the Barons* to his secretary, whilst occasionally ringing a bell to summon from the shore a faithful servant with food and refreshments. The lake, now a sanctuary for wildfowl, lies just out of sight across the fields as we pass, but in the deep and mysterious silence of the valley I have sometimes sworn I could hear Lord Lytton's bell ring out over the summer air!

On leaving High Barnet station turn left and follow the approach road up to the main road. Cross this to a path – slightly left of opposite – which descends a grassy embankment to a road junction. Turn left in the road, then go right on a path descending between flats and the Old Red Lion inn to another road. A path opposite leads beside the Barnet Football Club stadium to a playing field. Cross the field slightly leftwards to a transverse drive: from here a forward path takes you on down the left edge of the field to a path junction beside the Dollis Brook. Turn left now and follow the brookside path, beside housing at first, then along the green floor of the valley for three-quarters of a mile to a road. Here we are joined by newcomers leaving Totteridge and Whetstone station.

All walkers now turn right and follow the main road downhill for some 100 yards to a brookside path, signposted 'Finchley', beginning on the left. Keep by the stream, ignoring a narrow, railed footbridge over it, but at a broad slab bridge later the main path crosses the stream and resumes along its right bank to a road. Go right the full length of the road (Laurel Way) through a modern part of Totteridge. At the top of the hill a short path leads rightward to a pond at Totteridge Green, a picturesque spot with Laurel Farm to your left.

Keeping the pond on your left, follow the narrow track leading round it to its far side, keeping left to a corner. From here an enclosed path drops downhill to a stile, where keep downhill on a broad track running between fields, cross a brook at the bottom of the hill and continue uphill now for half a mile. After picking up wooden fencing, right, the broad track ends at a gateside stile giving on to a lane. Keep forward – along the lane at first, then along a road – until, after following the road uphill, you reach a point where the main road appears ahead: here fork sharply left to reach Mill Hill Ridgeway opposite the Adam and Eve inn.

Go right in the main road, and in a quarter of a mile turn right on a drive signposted to Totteridge Common and leading down the right side of St Vincent's School (Damascus House) over a stile. Just beyond a statue leave the drive for a fenced track leading to the foot of the field on your right and continuing past stables to a stile. Climb this, and another over to your right, and head diagonally down the length of a field to a stile in its bottom right-hand corner. Cross a drive and a second stile and resume direction across a playing field (or, if play is in progress, turn left around it) to a narrow gap halfway along the hedge to your left (i.e. facing the pavilion). Pass through the gap and keep straight on across another playing field (or, if play is in progress here, go rightwards around it) to its bottom right-hand corner. From here a clear path takes you along the foot of the next field to a crossing path, where turn left to the gates of Folly Farm.

Go right now beside the Folley Brook, cross a stile and plank bridge on emerging into the open, and follow a path half-left across a wide field. Go over a stile at a corner and continue along an enclosed path, with Darlands Lake lying just out of sight across the field to your right. In half a mile the path emerges at Totteridge village: just to your right – where The Darlands now stands – stood Copped Hall, while opposite is the eighteenth-century parish church, with its ancient yew tree, reputed to be a thousand years old, standing before its front porch.

Turn left in the road past the old village pound, marked by a memorial *c.*1560 by the gate of Pound House, fork left at the war

The Mitre, Barnet.

memorial and, 200 yards beyond it, turn right through a wooden gate on a footpath signposted to May's Lane. Follow the path downhill for half a mile, crossing a drive and a cul-de-sac and, finally, the Dollis Brook before climbing to a housing estate on the outskirts of Barnet. Keep straight on up the road to a main road. Turn right for a few yards, then left, opposite shops, on a path which climbs uphill past tennis courts and allotments. After a right-and-left twist the path runs straight on again through a play area and garden to a road at Chipping Barnet. Turn right past Barnet church, with the red-brick Tudor Hall, the original grammar school founded by Elizabeth I, on your right.

Most of the High Street lies to your left, but to complete the walk, follow it rightward (forward) down Barnet Hill, passing the Mitre, left, where General Monk stayed when he led his army into London to welcome Charles II at the Restoration. High Barnet station lies a quarter of a mile down on the left.

TRANSPORT

High Barnet station: Underground (Northern Line). *Totteridge & Whetstone station:* Underground (Northern Line). *Motorists:* direct service High Barnet to Totteridge & Whetstone by Underground (one station on Northern Line).

10. Off to see the windmill

Full round from Mill Hill (Old Forge or Three Hammers inn) or Arkley (Gate inn): 6¼ miles. Shorter round from Mill Hill (Old Forge or Three Hammers inn), omitting Arkley and windmill: 4 miles.

Anyone who has ever seen a working windmill, its sails whirling in full splendour as they swivel round to face each changing wind, will readily sympathise with poor Don Quixote, who mistook the windmills of his native Spanish landscape for giants! Here is a fine circular walk which takes us out to Arkley on the Hertfordshire border to see a typically English – and, of course, harmless – windmill. No longer working – it 'retired' as long ago as 1916 – it stands in its own very beautiful private garden near the Gate inn at Arkley, and the way there lies by the long tracks over the green Totteridge and Dollis valleys, where the yellowhammer sings and the kestrel hovers, and along the Totteridge Common ridge road. There is another glimpse to be had of the old village of Mill Hill, and I have devised a rather cunning manoeuvre at Arkley whereby we cross the fields to come suddenly and delightfully upon the windmill from the rear, an outflanking movement worthy of the Knight of the Woeful Figure himself!

St Paul's church, Mill Hill.

44

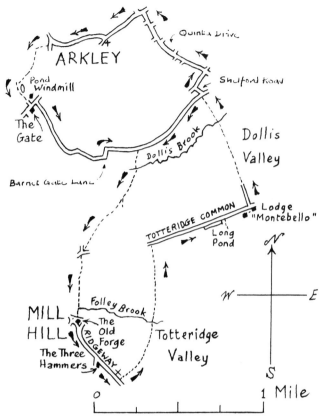

From the Old Forge, Mill Hill, ascend the ramp 30 yards right of the forge and go right along The Ridgeway, Mill Hill's fine old village street. Note, right, St Mary's Abbey (a Franciscan convent) and Holcombe House, once the home of Mr Druce, the Baker Street antique-furniture dealer. Just before Belmont – a house built reputedly by the Adam brothers and now a preparatory school for Mill Hill School – turn in to the Mill Field, right, believed by some to be the site of the mill which gave the village its name. From here on a clear day enthusiasts armed with telescopes can pick out Hindhead, forty miles away in Surrey! Keep to the path (which runs parallel with the road) and at the next gate resume along The Ridgeway.

Pass the Three Hammers inn, right; those unfamiliar with The Ridgeway, and perhaps wishing to explore it a little further than this walk allows, may refer to directions from the inn given in Walk 7. In any event, just beyond St Paul's church and school, left, turn left through a gate on to a path which crosses the beautiful Totteridge valley and in three-quarters of a mile reaches the ridge road at Totteridge Common.

Turn right and follow the sunken footpath left of the road, keeping a look-out in a quarter of a mile for the picturesque Long Pond (the second of two ponds, right), which has a narrow track running beside it along which progress may now be made. Some 300 yards beyond the pond – opposite the entrance lodge to Montebello, right – go left on a drive signposted to May's Lane. When this ends go over a stile and keep straight on down the left edge of two fields, and on again through more fields, following the telegraph poles until they end at a stile and plank bridge over the Dollis Brook.

Cross, and follow the left hedge forward to a road. Those doing the shorter round back to Mill Hill should turn left here and follow the road through the farmlands for half a mile to a stile by a gate, left, and situated just short of a house (Allendale). This will put them back on the route of the full round, directions for which will be found later in this ramble. To resume the walk to Arkley turn right in the road, immediately left along Shelford Road, and right along Greenland Road. At a road junction turn left and follow Quinta Drive all the way up to the Barnet Road at Arkley. Turn left along this to the war memorial, where fork right along Rowley Green Road to reach its junction with Rowley Lane at a concrete water-tower. Turn left for a few yards, then right on an enclosed path (signposted to Ripon Way, etc) which starts left of cottages.

Climb a stile on your left by a disused farmyard, and another on your left in a few yards, and cross a large field half-right to a stile by a small pond. This gives on to an enclosed track which affords good views of Borehamwood over to your right and suddenly the windmill can be seen through the hedge on your left. Keep forward with the hedge on your left to a sharp left turn. Go left and the windmill is just visible above the hedge, the white cap carrying the whirling sails being the part which turned whenever the wind veered.

Continue out to the road by the Gate inn.The sign once affixed to the toll-gate gave the inn its name:

'This gate hangs well
And hinders none
Refresh and pay
And travel on.'

46

The Long Pond, Totteridge.

Turn left and then right down Barnet Gate Lane. Follow the lane through the Dollis valley farmlands for three-quarters of a mile to a stile, right, and situated just beyond a house called Allendale.

This is the stile to which those doing the shorter round were referred earlier, and all walkers now go over this and head across a field to another stile. Recross the Dollis Brook by another stile and follow a forward path along the right edge of two fields, through a gate and across to a rough bridge by a stile in a corner. Go over the bridge and cut off the left corner of a playing field to reach a stile hidden in the hedge – look for a waymark post – 50 yards to its right. Veer slightly right across the next field to a hedge-gap and across a rough bridge in the diagonally opposite corner. (This path is not a public right of way and a small sign advises that, while walkers may proceed, the path will be closed for one day each year, usually 28th February.) Maintain direction across the next field to a gate in its top right-hand corner.

This gives on to a road junction: cross to a signposted stile opposite and follow the wooded track to another stile. Keep forward by the left hedge (through which there is a fine view over the Totteridge valley to the distant television mast of Alexandra Palace) and when this turns away left keep forward downhill past a tree-girt pond, left (the source of the Folley Brook), to a roadside stile at Mill Hill. Opposite is the Old Forge, where we began.

47

11. Rhododendron glory

Full walk from Borehamwood (Elstree station) to Mill Hill Broad-way station: 6¹/₄ miles. Shorter walk from Borehamwood (Elstree station) to Highwood Hill (Rising Sun inn): 4¹/₄ miles.

Nothing remains now of the great forest which once covered the counties of Middlesex, Hertfordshire and Essex except a fragment or two of woodland on London's northern border. Yet one of these, Scratch Wood, must surely make up in beauty for much that has been lost to progress, for it is a woodland paradise and should not be missed in late spring when its countless rhododendrons are bursting into flower, setting the woods ablaze with their glory. Here is a walk I take every year at this wonderful time, dropping down into Scratch Wood from Woodcock Hill (with its fine view over Hertfordshire) and breaking off later at Stirling Corner. Over the rolling fields of Moat Mount, my way leads on to the remains of its Victorian mansion, destroyed by a pre-war fire but once the home of the magazine king E. W. Cox, founder of *The Lady* and *The Field*. Mote End Farm was once owned by William Wilberforce; and it was at Highwood House that Sir Stamford Raffles spent the last year of his life on his return from Singapore.

The walk begins in the bustling Hertfordshire town of Borehamwood, known for its film and television studios. On leaving Elstree station keep right over the crossroads at the New Crown and on along Borehamwood's main shopping street, Shenley Road. Turn right along Furzehill Road and follow this for three-quarters of a mile to the top of a hill. Opposite a modern church (over to your left) go over a stile, right, signposted to Barnet Lane. Follow the track beside wire fencing through a meadow, and eventually on to a road. Turn left here for 100 yards and rejoin the wire fence at the footpath signposted 'Footpath 9'.

This is Woodcock Hill, and a little to your right a fine view is obtainable across Hertfordshire to the Chiltern Hills fifteen miles away. Follow the hedgeside track to a road. Go left in this – it forms the Hertfordshire-Greater London border – but in 200 yards, just beyond a house called Crosskeys by a post box, turn off right on a fenced track sweeping down beside a field to Scratch Wood.

On entering the wood turn right on a clear path, in a few yards turning right on a crossing track, with rhododendron bushes on your right. Keep forward along this track as it plays hide-and-seek with the right edge of the wood; but when the meadows on your right come to an end, and a garden screened by conifer trees

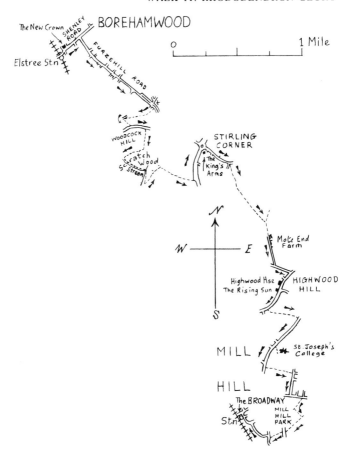

begins, look out in 50 yards for a left fork which carries you downhill into a beautiful valley.

Turn left beside the stream (sometimes dried up) which runs through the valley, and, keeping this right, follow it down the valley to a small footbridge and follow the clear path left to the stream's confluence with a larger rivulet. Cross this, turn right beside it, and in 50 yards or so keep forward on a clear path which climbs the higher ground slightly to your left. When this bends round left do not be lured out into the open, but turn left again on a

49

track running uphill just inside the right edge of the wood to a crossing track on the far side of the wood. Turn right now, towards conifers, passing waymark posts 12 and 13, and keep on beside the left hedge all the way to the main road. Turn uphill to the roundabout at Stirling Corner and the King's Arms inn.

Go right along the Barnet Road, and in a quarter of a mile turn right over a signposted stile just left of the entrance drive to Hyver Hall. Cross a field (keeping near the drive at first) to a plank bridge and stile just left of a wide hedge-gap. Cross, and go forward by a right hedge to a hedge gap in a corner. Through this, keep forward for a few more yards (ignoring a hedge gap, left), then veer half-left down a large sloping field (or follow its right edge) to its bottom right-hand corner. Keep ahead in the next field to a gateside stile on its top edge and turn right over this to follow a left hedge to another gateside stile at Mote End Farm.

Keep forward along the lane, passing in a few yards, right, the drive to the two-storey servants' quarters, cupola-topped chapel and single-storey stables, all that now remains of Moat Mount. When the lane ends go left along another lane to a road at Highwood Hill. Turn right, soon passing Highwood House and the seventeenth-century Rising Sun inn, and keep forward down Marsh Lane.

Scratch Wood open space.

The Rising Sun, at the end of the Ridgeway, Mill Hill.

In 300 yards, just before Marsh Close, left, go left on an enclosed path, signposted to Lawrence Street, which later descends through allotments, from which there is a fine view of the heights of Mill Hill, the squat steeple being that of St Mary's Abbey, a Franciscan convent on The Ridgeway. Go right in the road for half a mile. Just beyond Uphill Grove, right, go left on a path leading between fields. To your left is St Joseph's missionary college, its campanile topped by a gilded statue of the saint holding the infant Jesus in his arms. Turn right in a road, then left in a main road. Opposite Marion Road, left, enter Mill Hill Park by a path which passes a children's play area. At a park junction go left between a pavilion and a bowling green, and on past tennis courts to the second of the two crossing paths. Turn right, and with the domed buildings of London University Observatory soon appearing through the trees, right, follow the path through a tunnel and on to a road. Turn right, immediately left along Woodland Way, and at the end of this, left to Mill Hill Broadway station and the Broadway.

TRANSPORT
Borehamwood (Elstree station): British Rail Thameslink Line from London. *Mill Hill Broadway station:* British Rail Thameslink Line from London. *Motorists:* direct service Mill Hill Broadway to Borehamwood (Elstree) by British Rail, Thameslink Line (one station).

51

12. An Idle Street idyll

Full round from Stanmore station or Stanmore Broadway: 8¹/₂ miles. Shorter walk from Stanmore Hill (Vine inn) to Spur Road Roundabout or Canons Corner: 6³/₄ or 7 miles.

Not many folk know that Elstree, the ridge-top village partly in Greater London and partly in Hertfordshire, was once called Idle Street, a derivation from its ancient name of Idulfstre! Even today Elstree can still be a delightfully sleepy village, and despite some modern intrusions it is still a joy to come upon from the surrounding fields. Here, then, is something of an Idle Street idyll, a walk best taken in summer when the footpaths across the ploughed fields are firm and dry underfoot. Included in my 'idyll' are the wood-fringed Aldenham Reservoir – habitat of anglers, sailing enthusiasts and wildfowl – and old Stanmore, surely one of the prettiest spots in north London's countryside! Stanmore's pride is one of the loveliest of all commons; while among its ponds is the 'stony mere' which gave the village its name and is said to have been dug to provide water for a nearby Roman encampment.

On leaving Stanmore station turn left and follow the London Road to crossroads where it meets Stanmore Broadway. At this point turn up Dennis Lane and, at the top of the hill, follow the road round left to reach the beautiful village pond at old Stanmore, believed by many to have been the 'mere' of Roman times.

Those starting from the Vine inn, Stanmore Hill, will find this pond just along the road running right of the small green beside the inn, and all walkers now turn along the little path leading between the pond and cottages. Just beyond these turn squarely left along a track and, on gaining a gravelled, cottage-lined road, turn right along it to its far end.

From here a metalled path bends left and runs beside the common. Just where it meets a road, a track branches off right to run along the left edge of a birch-fringed reservoir. When the lake starts curving round right, break away from it – i.e. keep forward – through trees lining the right edge of a playing field. Cross a road and continue opposite on a clear track leading through the woods to a drive. Go right on this, then, keeping a sharp look-out for horse-riders, turn right and follow left fencing to a road.

Continue along the track opposite which runs slightly rightward away from the fence and shortly bends right beside more fencing to reach another road. Go left in this to hospital gates. A few yards to their left is a smaller gate: pass through this and follow an enclosed

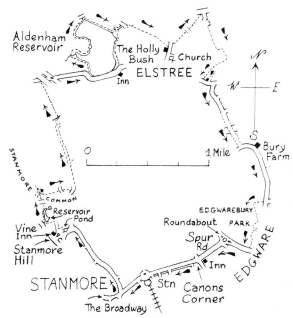

path downhill beside the hospital grounds and alongside a riding school. On a right bend go left over stiles and on down a lane. Do not bend sharp right with the lane but keep forward 50 yards or so to the stream ahead. Cross this (into Hertfordshire) and keep straight on through the next field to a gate on the Elstree road.

Go right now under the M1 motorway bridge, past the round-about and on along the forward road (i.e. second right). Just beyond a sharp right bend look for a track on your left and follow it leftwards into the woods lining the shore of Aldenham Reservoir. (See end of next paragraph.) The winding track follows the left edge of the woods, with fields often visible, left, and if this simple rule is remembered walkers will find themselves free to go off exploring in any direction they choose as they proceed through this lakeside wonderland.

In three-quarters of a mile, the woods peter out and the path leads past a children's adventure area and out on to a car park and picnic area. Continue beside the lake to the footbridge at the left end of the embankment which dams its northern shore. Turn right over it and along the embankment footpath, and when this ends keep forward along the main path which, beyond gates, becomes a

Aldenham Reservoir.

drive running out to a road. (Note: should access to the woods lining the western shore of the reservoir at any time be prevented, keep along the road and, 50 yards beyond the Fishery inn, turn left on a path running up the eastern shore, with the lake on your left. On reaching the above-mentioned drive turn right to the road.)

Cross the road and the stile opposite, and follow left fencing for 50 yards to where a faint track eases half-right in the direction of the ridge leftward of Elstree parish church. The track runs right of a solitary horse-chestnut tree, through a swing-gate at the right edge of the field, straight ahead through another gate (in left fencing) and straight on uphill to emerge at a road at Elstree just left of the Holly Bush inn. A secret passage is supposed to have led from this pleasant fifteenth-century inn to St Albans Abbey, while nearby are other picturesque buildings including the parish church of St Nicholas.

Take the path which begins at the war memorial (a few yards downhill) and follow it down into a valley and up again to a main road. Ignore the road, turn back right on a farm lane and, when this bends right, leave it over a stile to follow the right edge of a field all the way to its bottom right-hand corner. Cross over a double stile and go directly across the field to a plank bridge 50 yards left of the right-hand corner, and cross another stile. Follow a right hedge forward the length of the field on your immediate right to its top left-hand corner. Turn right and climb the left edge of this sloping field until the left fencing ends at a corner commanding fine views.

Go forward now on a woodland track winding along the edge of grounds belonging to the red-brick house seen shortly to your left. On reaching a road (forming the Hertfordshire-Greater London border) head uphill to the Edgewarebury Hotel and Edgwarebury Lane. Follow this downhill and, with fine southerly views ahead, cross the M1 motorway to reach a transverse lane at the chalet-·style Edgwarebury Farm. Go left on this, soon passing Bury Farm, but opposite Hartland Drive in half a mile (soon after the lane becomes a residential road) turn off right on a metalled path leading into Edgwarebury Park.

Keep forward over grass beside a left hedge, and, when this ends, turn left to go beside a right hedge to reach a metalled path. Go right on this, left around the far end of tennis courts, then right on a crossing path (a floral roundabout with an oak tree) all the way through the park to a road. Go right to a roundabout, where turn left into Spur Road (signposted to Stanmore, etc). The walk can be finished at bus stops here; alternatively keep on along this main road to reach Canons Corner in a quarter of a mile, Stanmore station in three-quarters of a mile, or Stanmore Broadway in one mile.

TRANSPORT
Stanmore station: Underground (Jubilee Line).

Elstree parish church.

55

VINe (STANMORE HIll)
VINTRY - CHurch St ?

13. The eagle's eyrie

Full round from Stanmore station or Stanmore Broadway: 6¹/4 or 5³/4 miles. Shorter round from Bushey Heath (Alpine Restaurant), omitting Stanmore: 4¹/4 miles.

The stirring days of the Battle of Britain are brought to mind on this fine ramble through the glorious birchwoods of Harrow Weald and Stanmore Commons, for towards the end of it we are close to Bentley Priory, the great house at Stanmore which became the headquarters of RAF Fighter Command during that titanic struggle. From this secluded eyrie, set in its own beautiful parklands, Air Chief Marshal Dowding summoned forth his young eagles to challenge and overthrow the might of Hitler's Luftwaffe, performing a service to Britain that drew from Sir Winston Churchill the immortal tribute: 'Never in the field of human conflict was so much owed by so many to so few.'

On leaving Stanmore station go left along the main road, which later becomes Stanmore Broadway. At Lloyds Bank turn right up Stanmore Hill. Just beyond the Abercorn Arms (and before a road junction, left) turn left on a pathway alongside a brick building, signposted to Green Lane, and on past a small green. Cross a road and take the enclosed path opposite, which later becomes a road dropping downhill to a field. Take the forward metalled path, over a cross path, following the sign to Clamp Hill. Cross a wooden plank bridge on the far side and ease right along a fence-side path.

When this finally runs into a farm lane keep forward along it to a road. Turn right in this, and just beyond Brickfield Cottage in 150 yards go left on an enclosed path. Turn right in another road and in 100 yards go left along Brookshill Drive. Follow it round right, and just beyond White Cottage (with its pretty view) climb a stile, right, and follow the right edge of a field to another stile. Cross this, go left beside left fencing to a road, and turn left.

Unless diverting for refreshments to the Case Is Altered inn 100 yards further on, turn right almost immediately on a broad track leading through the birchwoods of Harrow Weald Common. At a junction of paths near a half-timbered cottage, twist left and right to pick up a left fence belonging to cottages. Now keep straight on along this beautiful path as first it skirts the left edge of the wood, then – when the wood broadens out to your left – plunges forward through the trees to a road. Go left along this to crossroads at Bushey Heath.

The Alpine Restaurant, Windmill inn and bus stops (for those

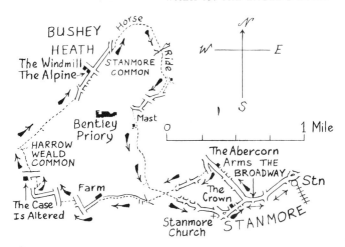

finishing the walk here) are to your left but, for the full walk, continue opposite along Magpie Hall Road, noting at a road junction shortly the house County End, standing on the Greater London-Hertfordshire border. Turn right now into Hathbourne Road and immediately left over tree trunk barriers to a horse path and the birch-woods of Stanmore Common, its wild interior honeycombed with footpaths along which many delightful hours may be spent in leisurely wandering. For swift and sure navigation, however, use the horse-ride as your guide (without actually walking on it), taking any one of the nearby paths and keeping the ride fairly close by your left hand, either by sight or by sound of the thudding hooves of the riders passing along it. In three-quarters of a mile the ride runs into a crossing drive, on which turn right to a road.

Go right in this, cross a main road, and continue opposite along a road lined with gracious homes. At a crossing road turn right, and at a right bend go through a gate, left, and follow the path leading through the deer park of Bentley Priory, the eighteenth-century mansion surmounted by its clock-tower away on the right. In a good half-mile, and with houses now appearing ahead, those doing the shorter round turn right on a grassy crossing track signposted to Clamp Hill, cross a wooden plank bridge on the far side of the field and ease right along a fence-side path, further directions being found near the beginning of this ramble.

The rest keep forward to a road, and on along this to a main road. Go left in this past Stanmore church, in its grounds the ivy-covered ruins of the old church, abandoned in 1845 on account of its

Stanmore old church.

dangerous condition. Pass the Crown inn, left, the main road soon becoming Stanmore Broadway and then the London Road, which leads on to the station.

TRANSPORT

Stanmore station: Underground (Jubilee Line).

14. A trip to Titipu

From Bushey station to Pinner station: 7¹/₄ miles.

This is a trip to the town of Titipu, where the Mikado held court, Ko-Ko proclaimed of the punishment that fits the crime, and Nanki-Poo prepared to die for his love of the beautiful Yum-Yum! It is, of course, Grim's Dyke, the many-gabled mansion on the edge of Harrow Weald Common where the great W. S. Gilbert lived for twenty years and where the last of the Gilbert and Sullivan operettas were written. Today it is run as a luxury hotel; but even if walkers do not visit the house for luncheon, they may still wander among the rhododendrons and azaleas of Grim's Dyke's beautiful grounds, and stroll along the drive down which Gilbert came on that morning in 1911 to meet his death in his garden swimming pool whilst in the gallant act of saving a lady guest from drowning. Our trip takes in two lovely old churches, gracing two ancient high streets, Bushey and Pinner. An added attraction for those who come on a weekday will, with any luck, be a glimpse of the Suzanne's Riding School blacksmith at work at his forge.

Grim's Dyke, Harrow.

The walk begins in Hertfordshire at Bushey station: leave by the Bushey exit, cross to the Railway Arms and walk along the Aldenham Road to traffic lights. Turn right along the main road. Just before a green, turn right down Haydon Road. At the end of this go through a gate and continue forward through a field, soon picking up on your left a hedge of hawthorn trees, which you keep close beside you for a while. On reaching a footbridge turn left over it, and follow the little path round right to a road. Cross to an enclosed path opposite and follow it to a crossing path.

Climb left on this through the churchyard of St James the Apostle, famous for its many complicated (and lovely) bell chimes, to reach Bushey High Street. (There are inns to your right.) Retrace your steps now through the churchyard, this time keeping straight on along the footpath to a road. Go left in this, but in half a mile – beyond some schools and just before Victoria Road on the left – go right on a path, signposted to Oxhey Lane, which drops down Merry Hill beside a right hedge. Ignore a left fork shortly, and when the path finally ends (at a gate) keep absolutely straight ahead down a field to reach a roadside stile near its bottom right-hand corner.

Go left in the road but, at a road junction in half a mile, climb over a stile by a gate near a pylon, left (signposted 'Grim's Dyke'), and cross two stiles over two fields. In 300 yards you should converge with the hedge on your right at a stile situated under the last of a line of oak trees. Cross this and follow a left hedge – round the edge of a golf course – to a cottage. You are now in Greater London. Go left around the cottage to a lane and follow it out to a road.

Cross the road and go forward into the wood opposite beside right fencing. When this turns away right, turn squarely left and make your way through the trees to the road. Go forward into the birchwoods of Harrow Weald Common opposite, keeping near left fencing. This runs along a low embankment, built by Sir W. S. Gilbert to mark the boundary of Grim's Dyke; soon this bends right, and a little further on those who wish will find opportunity to roam among the beautiful trees and shrubs, some of them quite rare, lying to the left. For the walk, however, keep just right of the embankment (ignore the fencing, some of which may have been removed or diverted) and when in a quarter of a mile the embankment starts to bend right again (to drop to the road) turn left over it, then at once go right on a little path running through the rhododendrons to a drive.

This was Gilbert's drive: turn left (for the hotel), afterwards making your way back along the beautiful drive to the road. Before turning left to the Case Is Altered inn, however, it is worth going

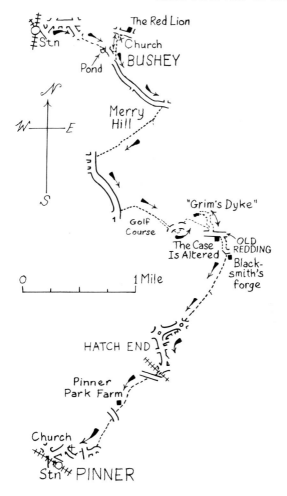

out on to the viewpoint opposite for fine southerly views over Harrow and the surrounding district, Harrow-on-the-Hill church being a distinctive feature on its lofty height.

Just beyond the inn a fenced drive runs rightward to cottages and riding stables but, when it bends sharply left to climb uphill, leave it to continue forward on a track, signposted to Oxhey Lane, which

The Case is Altered, Stanmore.

passes the shed, left, housing the blacksmith's forge, then bears half-right downhill, first beside a right hedge then a left hedge. When the latter ends at a swing-gate maintain direction along a fenced track to a roundabout. Go round this and on along the forward road (i.e. third exit), keeping to the cottage-lined service road on its left side (Boniface Walk).

At the next roundabout follow the little road round left and, when it runs into a side road, keep forward along the main road. Fork right past the Letchford Arms, following the road round right to cross the railway line by a footbridge. Go forward over a lane and on along a fenced track, which later leads past the buildings of Pinner Park Farm and on to another road. Continue along the track opposite, which climbs to a road at Pinner. Bear right downhill to a crossing road.

Take the enclosed path beginning just right of opposite, and in the next road go right to Pinner's fourteenth-century church. Turn left down the beautiful High Street, with its ancient houses and inns, and at the foot of this either turn right for bus stops, or go left and quickly left again up the approach road to Pinner station.

TRANSPORT

Bushey station: British Rail from Euston. *Pinner station:* Underground (Metropolitan Line).

15. Dispensatio fidelis

Round trip from Kenton station or Northwick Park station: 4 or 3¹/₂ miles.

Donorum Dei dispensatio fidelis runs the motto of Harrow School, meaning 'A faithful stewardship of the gifts of God'. Churchill, Palmerston, Peel, Shaftesbury, Sheridan, Byron, Trollope, Galsworthy, Cardinal Manning – the list of Harrovians whose 'faithful stewardship' was to earn them a place in Britain's history is long indeed! Many walkers will enjoy a visit to the ancient school from which has stemmed so much of the flower of Britain's greatness, and to the old village on the hill, in its charmingly rural setting – where its venerable buildings stand. We shall take in the Speech Room, to which Churchill would joyously return in his great days to sing the old school songs, and St Mary's church, in its yard the Peachey Stone on which the schoolboy Byron would lie, 'dreaming poetry all alone' and gazing out at a view over thirteen counties.

On leaving Kenton station go left in the main road, then take the second left turn (Rushout Avenue). At the bottom turn right to Northwick Park station. All walkers now take the passageway (to Northwick Park Hospital) leading under the railway line and at once turn left on a metalled path running along the right edge of a playing field (Proyer's Path). When the right-hand fencing ends turn right with it (over a ditch) on to a pitch and putt golf course and keep beside it again, the fence-side track later passing right of a wood and finally swinging left through it to the Watford road.

Go right for 250 yards, then left along a broad track running between the Harrow School playing fields. Ignore a lane on your right in a quarter of a mile, but in a few more yards turn right up Football Lane, signposted 'Public footpath to Peterborough Hill'. There are double gates as well as a stile at its entrance. Climb past the school Music Room and new and old Science Rooms to the village of Harrow-on-the-Hill. All around you are the buildings of Harrow School.

Keep left in the main road: to your right is the Speech Room (assembly hall), on its wall a statue of Queen Elizabeth I, under whose royal charter the school was founded in 1572 by John Lyon, a local yeoman. At this point turn back right along Grove Hill where, in a few yards is a plaque on the wall of the Art School, left, indicating that Charles I paused here in his flight from Oxford to Nottingham. Just beyond this turn left to mount steps and climb a

The Old Schools Building, Harrow-on-the-Hill.

Plaque commemorating Charles I's visit and a bust of Hogarth on the Art School, Harrow School.

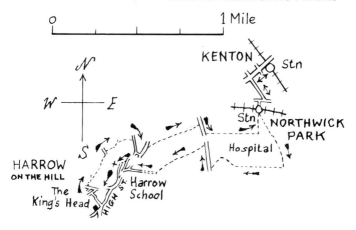

footpath leading to Church Hill. On your right is The Grove, once Sheridan's home and now one of the school's dozen houses. Walk past the back of the semicircular Speech Room, the regimental flags of the school's nineteen winners of the Victoria Cross hanging within; a lychgate, right, leads to St Mary's church, its tower part-Norman, and – beyond its porch – to a bronze plate pointing out the magnificent view to the west. Nearby, protected now by railings, lies the tombstone of John Peachey immortalised by Byron.

Resuming along Church Hill, note the red-brick building with a clock-tower, right, on its wall a plaque dedicated to Lord Shaftesbury: this was the original school house, built in 1615 (after John Lyon's death), and among the boyhood names carved on the oak panelling within are those of four of Harrow's seven prime ministers.

Continuing down to the High Street note, left, the school chapel and Vaughan library, both by Sir George Gilbert Scott, and, right, Druries, another of the school houses. Keep forward along the beautiful High Street, with its eighteenth- and nineteenth-century houses, in 300 yards passing, left, The Park, a school house built originally for Lord Northwick. Now the way lies right down little Waldron Road, but first note, in the Square before you, the school outfitters (where the famous wide-brimmed straw hat may be bought) and the King's Head, parts of which (although not the façade) date back to 1535.

At the foot of winding Waldron Road turn right, then left in a crossing road. In 80 yards go right along an alleyway signposted

'The Hill and Harrow', then take the track – rather faint at times – leading half-right up the centre of the hill. At the top twist right and left to pass along the foot of St Mary's churchyard. Turn left into a cul-de-sac, then immediately right along an enclosed path. When this runs out into the open keep forward a few more yards, then strike right (over grass) beside a wood and keep straight on to a road. Climb right in this, take the first left turn (Davidsons Lane), go left in another road, then – in 100 yards – turn off on an enclosed path, right, which runs between fields to the Watford road.

Go right for 100 yards, then turn left on an enclosed path which strikes between university and hospital buildings and leads all the way back to Northwick Park station. Continue under the railway line, those returning to Kenton station retracing their steps up Rushout Avenue and turning right in the main road.

TRANSPORT
Kenton station: British Rail from Euston; Underground (Bakerloo Line). *Northwick Park station:* Underground (Metropolitan Line).

John Peachey's tomb in the churchyard at Harrow-on-the-Hill.

16. Borderland beauty

Round trip from High Barnet station: 7 miles.

Borderland walks always seem to be among the most beautiful of all, and the one chosen here is no exception, starting and finishing in Chipping Barnet's historic old town and taking us out, by way of leafy Arkley Lane, to Dyrham Park just over the Hertfordshire border. Our route leads us round the lovely wooded perimeter of the estate, now a golf course but once the home of the philanthropist John Trotter. Old Fold Golf Course, traversed on the way back, was the scene of the Earl of Oxford's attack on Lord Hastings in the battle of Barnet.

Those wishing to visit Barnet's seven-hundred-year-old market, or chipping, held on Wednesdays and Saturdays, will find opportunity to do so towards the end of the walk, which begins at High Barnet station. Turn right on leaving the station and climb the approach path to the road above. Keep forward up the High Street. At traffic lights fork left along Wood Street, passing between Barnet church and, left, the red-brick Tudor Hall, the original grammar school founded by Elizabeth I. Beyond the Black Horse, right, the road may be avoided for a while by diverting through a park, regaining Wood Street via a side road at the end of the dried-up pond.

At the Arkley inn fork right along Galley Lane and when this bends right go left along a broad-walk which skirts the ancient Three Elms Farm, right, and runs between hedges to a road. Keep forward in this to a crossing lane (Arkley Lane), where turn right. Follow this beautiful lane for a good mile – it becomes a track beyond a gate – and at a concrete footbridge over a stream (just beyond a sharp right bend) go over a stile on the right, signposted to Galley Lane.

Strike left across a field, aiming for the second pylon from the left, visible beyond the trees in the distance. Cross a ditch by a culvert (ignore a plank-bridge to its left) and follow a faint track half-right across a field, with Fold Farm ahead of you, to a hedge. Ease half-right to follow this along the left edge of the next field to a corner. Go left for a few yards to a gate on the right. Climb over this and strike half-left across a field to a hidden roadside stile in the left hedge. Go left in the road (past Fold Farm) and when, in 600 yards, a little bridge carries the road over a stream go right across a ditch on to a signposted path by the gates of Little Dyrham and enter Dyrham Park (and Hertfordshire).

Follow the beautiful path leading round the wooded right edge of the park, with open fields emerging later, left, the path never straying far from these even if it wanders uncertainly through the trees at times. When the fields give way to a golf course look across it for an occasional glimpse of the mansion built by John Trotter early in the nineteenth century. Later the path sweeps round right to an iron footbridge over a watercourse, and on to a hedge. Ease right beside the hedge, following it closely round the right edge of the park. Once outside the great gateway you follow the curving traffic road (Trotters Bottom) rightward to crossroads, then go right along the main St Albans road.

Half a mile beyond the Green Dragon, just before the road veers left go slightly left through a gap in the roadside hedge, signposted 'Footpath 63', and on up the left edge of a narrow thicket, with a large open field left. At the top of the hill scramble through such gaps as you may find in the thicket ahead and out on to Old Fold Golf Course. Keep forward but progress with care, passing right of bunkers, and at the top of the slope pick up a left hedge. The right-of-way across the course (later marked by black and white posts) now hugs the hedge, eases left with it, then, when the hedge ends, runs straight ahead through the open for 50 yards and on through a narrow gap to pick up another left hedge which it follows, absolutely straight ahead, to a crossing track (with black and white post and footpath sign).

Dyrham Park gateway.

CHIPPING (OR HIGH)
BARNET

Turn left (between hedges), and at another post in a few yards bear right beside a left hedge to another post. Now break off half-right over grass towards a plantation of oak saplings, and follow the green track running through it to another post. You are now back in Greater London. Keep forward to pass on your left the corner of a hedge, then ease slightly leftward beside a ditch, to a stile giving on to an enclosed track. Follow this to a signposted path junction, where turn back sharply right on a metalled path running right of houses. Keep forward on reaching a lane and, when this finally bends left, follow it round (ignoring the forward path) and on out to the main road at the south end of Hadley Green.

Go right along Chipping Barnet's High Street, with its many inns, soon passing the St Albans road, right, where the market is held. Bearing left past the church, note the Mitre, left, where General Monk stayed when he led his army into London to welcome Charles II at the Restoration. Keep on down Barnet Hill to High Barnet station.

TRANSPORT
High Barnet station: Underground (Northern Line).

17. Barnet's battlefield

Full round from New Barnet station, Cockfosters station or High Barnet station: 6¹/₂, 7 or 7¹/₄ miles. Shorter round from High Barnet station, omitting New Barnet and Cockfosters: 4¹/₂ miles.

No follower of these walks will wish to leave out the spot where Barnet's great battle of the roses was fought on Easter Day 1471; where Edward IV, the young Duke of York, vanquished his mortal enemy, Warwick the Kingmaker; and where the brave Earl of Oxford, hurrying back to the scene of battle after pursuing Hastings's men into Barnet, mistook his Lancastrian comrades in the fog for Yorkists, and to cries of 'Treason!' dealt them the 'stab in the back' that sank the whole Lancastrian cause. The little road leading from Monken Hadley, that jewel among Barnet villages, to lovely Hadley Green, where David Livingstone once lived, lay at the heart of the fighting; and we shall reach it after journeying over Monken Hadley's great common, known locally as Hadley Woods and famed far and wide for its beauty at all seasons.

Of the three stations serving the walk High Barnet (full round, 7¹/₄ miles) and Cockfosters (7 miles) will no doubt prove popular starting points, each being on the Underground, while New Barnet (6¹/₂ miles) has the advantage of entailing the minimum of road-walking at each end of the ramble. If starting at New Barnet station leave by the York Road exit and descend Station Road to the post office, where an alleyway drops to the main road. Go right under the railway bridge and past the Rat and Parrot inn.

Keep ahead now over the road junction and along Victoria Road. In 100 yards, at a small green on the left, a minor road descends to a recreation ground. Follow a lamp-posted path slightly rightward across the park to a crossing path on the far side. Turn right on this and follow it round, right of a children's play area, and at another crossing path turn left to a road.

Go right downhill to a T junction where turn left beside Pymme's Brook, walking on the green. Cross the road where it bends right and keep ahead by a narrow brookside path to a brick and rubble bridge on the edge of Monken Hadley Common. Turn right over this and keep straight ahead up the right edge of the common, at Ludgrove Hall (University of Middlesex) taking the forward road to wooden gates at the top of the hill. Unless finishing at Cockfosters station, or diverting to the Cock and Dragon inn for refreshments, turn back left on a green track running diagonally across the common, referred to again in the next paragraph. For the station

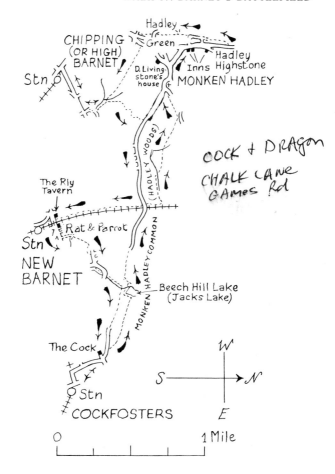

(and the inn) pass through the gates and down a road to a road junction, with the inn right. Opposite is Chalk Lane which runs with playing fields on its left to the parish church, where it bends left to the main road and station.

Those starting the walk at Cockfosters station should leave by the Hadley Wood exit and turn left, then immediately left again along Chalk Lane. At the parish church the lane bends right, then runs beside playing fields to a T junction. To your left is the Cock

Monken Hadley church.

and Dragon inn; continue along Games Road opposite and pass through gates on to Monken Hadley Common. From here a green track runs diagonally across the common to its far right side, through a gap in the holly, and on downhill near right-hand fencing, it mattering little which path you take from here so long as you keep downhill with the fencing fairly close at hand. In a while a woodland stream is picked up, and later, from a metal bridge, a path running downhill through the open to Beech Hill Lake, an artificial water known locally as Jacks Lake on account of its reputation for vast numbers of jacks (young pike).

Go left beside the lake and around the end of it to cross the bridge spanning the outflow into Pymme's Brook. In a few yards pick up a clear crossing path and sweep leftward through the trees to a wide crossing track on the edge of the common. Turn right along this: it soon runs across open common, then becomes a road winding uphill to a railway bridge.

All walkers now turn off beside wire fencing bordering the railway line, those doing the shorter round finding it on their left, those doing the full round crossing the bridge to find it on their right. Follow the fencing, with the railway right, all the way to a large clearing with houses beyond. Here bend round left with the path, ignoring a minor right fork through the trees in a few yards. Keep absolutely straight on this track until it runs beside a spring, right. Follow the spring for nearly half a mile until grassland can be seen beyond the wood. Keep your direction and head into the open to find yourself between two converging roads. Head straight ahead towards their intersection by the wooden gate right of the road junction and left of Monken Hadley church.

Go into the churchyard: I have rarely found the church open, but it should certainly be visited if it is, being nearly as old as the battle of Barnet itself. The beacon on its tower was lit for VE Day and the coronation of Queen Elizabeth II. Continue out to the beautiful village, noting its enclosure gate. Turning right in the road – once straddled by the opposing forces of Warwick's brother Montagu (facing you) and Edward – you come to a fork at Hadley Green, and it could not have been far from this spot that Montagu's archers turned and fired at Oxford as he came charging at them out of the fog. The way now lies right along Dury Road, but a short detour left along Hadley Green Road will bring you to David Livingstone's house.

Retrace your steps to Dury Road, all walkers now passing along this (with the green left) to a T junction. Turn right into Hadley Highstone. Pass the ancient King William IV inn, forking left shortly past the commemorative Highstone itself, said to mark the spot where Warwick was overtaken and slain as he walked to his horse in Wrotham Wood after the battle. Just beyond a red-brick house (Colebrooke Court, left) turn back sharply left on an enclosed path signposted 'Taylors Lane'. To your right is the golf course where Oxford attacked Hastings. Keep forward along a cottage-lined road, and forward still – when it turns away left – on a track running all the way down the right edge of Hadley Green to some cottages at the far end. Turn left here to the main road.

To your right is Chipping Barnet High Street (inns and restaurants) but, to continue the walk, cross the main road and green and turn left in the road beyond. In a few yards go right through a gate into a field. Follow the clear path across a stile and continue down-

Hadley Highstone, Barnet.

73

hill, keeping to the ridge all the way, with fine views ahead over New Barnet and beyond. At the foot of the hill cross a culvert but, unless finishing at High Barnet station, ignore a swing-gate just ahead of you and turn left instead up a narrow field, mentioned again in the next paragraph. For High Barnet station go ahead through the gate posts and retrace your outward steps, i.e. along the gravel track to a road, sharp right along the footpath and on along Burnside Close to crossroads, then right up Meadway to the station.

If commencing the walk at High Barnet station turn right on leaving it and climb the approach path to the road above. Turn right down Meadway. At crossroads in a long quarter-mile go left along Burnside Close and when this ends keep on along a short footpath to another road. Now go left on a gravel track running along the foot of a sloping field. Pass through gate posts and, ignoring the track running ahead through a gap, swing round right instead up a narrow field.

Ignore the first wide gap in the right hedge (where a corner is formed with another hedge), but veer half-right through the next wide gap on a faint green track running uphill to a playing field. Pass through the gate and go left around the left edge of the field until soon you come to a corner, from which a metalled path runs off left between hedges. Follow this hedged path out to a road on the edge of Monken Hadley Common. Go right along the road (there is a sunken footpath to its left) for half a mile, leaving the main road when it sweeps right, through gates, and continue forward down Bakers Lane to a railway bridge – but do not cross it. For the shorter round see directions from the bridge given earlier; for the full round turn right on a path running downhill beside wire fencing.

Follow this for half a mile to a road at New Barnet, a railway town that grew up around the station around 1900. If finishing at the station cross the road, mount the steps opposite and turn left in Station Road; if continuing the walk go left under the railway bridge and past the Rat and Parrot inn, further directions being found near the beginning of this ramble.

TRANSPORT

New Barnet station: British Rail from Moorgate, Monday to Friday, or King's Cross, Saturday and Sunday. *Cockfosters station*: Underground (Piccadilly Line). *High Barnet station*: Underground (Northern Line).

18. Trent Park

Full walk from Oakwood station to Cockfosters station: 4³/4 miles.
Short circuit from Cockfosters car park within Trent Park: 4 miles.

When, in 1968, the Sassoon family's association with Trent Park came to an end, this beautiful estate that had once been the seat of George III's physician, Sir Richard Jebb, was designated a Country Park, and the public gained possession of a truly magnificent heritage of grassland and lake and deep tracts of forest teeming with wildlife. Walking here is a delight, and in this easy-to-follow circumnavigation of Trent Park we shall take in almost every aspect of its varied charm, including the Fernyhill Farm Trail. So bring the family along, and provisions for a picnic in some broad meadow or silent forest glade.

The entrance to Trent Park, Enfield.

Chalk Lane + James Rd
THe COCK+
DRaga

On leaving Oakwood station cross the road to the entrance to Trent Park and follow the clear track forward, with the railway left. Soon the track runs through a wood and on along the left edge of a field. In the next field leave the railway to swing right downhill beside a right hedge. Hug the right hedge again in the next field, following the track round left later as it runs on between fields, with a ditch left. In a while the main track swings right to climb the edge of a wood. At the top turn right on a crossing track and ignore the next paragraph.

Motorists setting out on the short circuit from the Cockfosters car park within Trent Park should walk back past the obelisk at the car park entrance and, just beyond the junction with the avenue of lime trees leading to the great house, turn left on the Blind Persons' Trail. When the trail forks inside a wood keep left along its top edge, and continue straight ahead along this very beautiful track, ignoring all right turns, and past a sports pavilion.

At cottages later keep straight on over a crossing road and along the forward road, with a fine view opening up of Enfield dominated by the spire of St Mary's church and, on the far distant ridge, the towns of Chingford and Woodford and the fringes of Epping Forest. Among the buildings, left, some of which (like the mansion itself) now belong to the University of Middlesex , is the rambling white-walled villa with grey slate roof occupied until her recent

Trent Park house, Enfield.

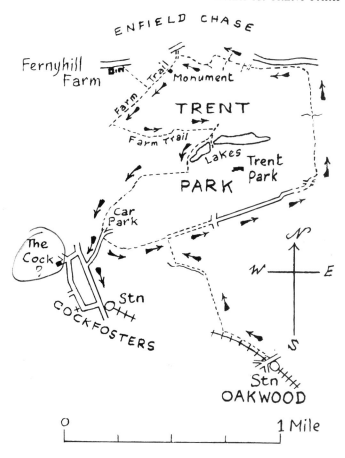

death by Mrs Gubbay, the last of the Sassoon family to live on the estate. During the Second World War Trent Park served as a prisoner-of-war camp and the captured Afrika Corps general von Thoma would often stop for a chat with the children who lived at the gabled house on your right (Northview).

In a while the pretty road becomes no more than a track running broadly through woodland: keep forward along it, through gates, ignoring any side tracks or cross-tracks (some of them horse-rides) as it winds on through the beautiful forest. Later the track veers round left to run parallel with a road. Keep forward still, over all crossing tracks, drives and horse-rides, until in nearly three-quarters of a mile the main track bends left beside an open field. In 150 yards a tall monument is reached, erected in memory of the Earl of Harold, son of the Duke of Kent, who died in infancy in 1702. It was brought here from Wrest Park, Bedfordshire, by Sir Philip Sassoon in 1933. Follow the path past the monument until it reaches an open field. Here turn sharp left and follow a fence-enclosed path by the side of a wood (a large water-tower is visible over the fields to the right) until you reach the bottom of the wood.

Now go forward over grass to reach the footpath seen running down to the lakes in the valley below at the point where it emerges from the sloping wood before you. From here a fine view of the great house of Trent Park, rebuilt in 1894, may be obtained. Turn right on the path and take the right fork, which runs near one of the lakes, then sweeps left round its far end. Turn uphill with it, but in 100 yards – opposite the entrance to the nature trail – turn right (to Cockfosters) and follow the main track on through a wood. After a while it swings round left and climbs gently for a quarter of a mile to a road at the Cockfosters car park entrance.

To complete the full walk keep forward on the road to the main road and, unless diverting to the Cock and Dragon inn for refreshments (adding a quarter of a mile to the walk), go left to Cockfosters station. For the inn turn right in the main road, then first left along Chalk Lane. From the inn the station may best be reached by turning sharp right along Chalk Lane (with playing fields left) to the parish church, where bend left with the lane to the main road.

TRANSPORT
Oakwood station: Underground (Piccadilly Line). *Cockfosters station:* Underground (Piccadilly Line). *Motorists:* direct service Cockfosters to Oakwood by Underground (one station on Piccadilly Line).

19. Through history and legend to Forty Hall

Round trip from Enfield (Gordon Hill station): 6¹/₄ miles.

A visit to Forty Hall, the elegant Jacobean mansion near Enfield, provides a grand climax to a walk. The debate still goes on as to whether it was Inigo Jones who built it for Sir Nicholas Raynton, a Lord Mayor of London; the house certainly bears some of the hallmarks of the great architect's style. Our route to Forty Hall winds through the intimately lovely countryside just north of Enfield, rich in history and in legends of the great royal hunting chase of which it once formed part. One story goes that the ancient Fallow Buck inn marks the spot where Henry VIII, then a young prince, slew his first buck; another that in the porchway of the King and Tinker James I, out on a hunt from nearby Theobalds, shared a jug of ale with an outspoken tinker whom he afterwards knighted in the greenwood close by:

> 'They drank to King Jamie,
> and pledged one another,
> Who'd seen 'em had thought
> they were brother and brother.'

The King and Tinker pub, near Enfield.

Our footsteps lead on beside the New River, truly a royal river for King James himself financed its construction to relieve London's water shortage, and past ancient Whitewebbs, standing on the site of a former house which the arch-plotter Guy Fawkes must almost certainly have known, for it was a nest of intrigue during the days of the Gunpowder Plot conspiracy.

On leaving Gordon Hill station turn left along Lavender Hill and follow this road all the way to The Ridgeway, in which go right. Pass Chase Farm Hospital on your right, and in a quarter of a mile, just before Oak Avenue, left, go right on a bridleway to Rectory Farm. Bend right with it around the farm, passing under a railway bridge, and when finally it ends at a crossing track go right. Soon the lane becomes a road, and later runs into a main road, with Clay Hill parish church left, and the Fallow Buck inn right.

Continue opposite along Flash Lane, the beautiful bridleway soon running downhill and on through woodland. A bridge carries it over the outflow from a lake, and the lane rises, narrowing now to a fenced track. In 150 yards – by a tree with a 'No horse-riding' sign – turn through the right-hand of twin exits opposite each other in the fencing. Follow a faint path which describes a gentle leftward curve through the trees to reach the holly bushes over to your left at a point some 80 yards in from the bridleway.

You should now be able to see a clear and straight track running

Forty Hall, Enfield.

on through the wood almost parallel to the bridleway. (If it is not clear and straight search again: there is no mistaking it!) Keep straight on along this little-known path through Whitewebbs Wood, disregarding any side tracks or cross-tracks. In a while it develops into a beautiful glade running ahead through the forest, finally ending at a metalled crossing drive. Continue opposite, ignoring the little path, and keeping straight on instead over grass beside a thicket, left. Finally bear left to a road in which go right to the King and Tinker inn.

Beyond the inn follow the right-hand footpath, which soon veers right to run on just alongside Whitewebbs Golf Course. When it ends turn right on a track running down the edge of the golf course between iron railings; in a while the old course of the New River – long since diverted – is picked up, left, and a little later the eighteenth-century mansion of Whitewebbs, now a retirement home, may be seen away right.

Just before the path crosses the Cuffley Brook on a bend, turn left through a very narrow gap by an old iron gatepost, and then immediately right, with an open field on your left. Cross a foot-bridge and turn left along the right bank, keeping beside the stream as it winds its wooded way beside fields. Later the rhododendrons of the Forty Hall home park line the track, while a lake accompanies you, right. Some 100 yards or so beyond the end of the lake, and when almost level with the remains of a bridge over the stream, go squarely right over grass between two double rows of lime trees leading up to Forty Hall.

On reaching a lakeside drive turn right and follow it all the way round to the mansion, passing the Jacobean archway (in the style of Inigo Jones) with its charming courtyard. After visiting the house and gardens – the walled flower garden was once the kitchen garden – resume your original direction, veering half-right now along a little track beginning at steps and running under the branches of a giant cedar of Lebanon to a roadside swing-gate in the bottom right-hand corner of the grounds.

Go right in the road (Forty Hill), keeping right past the Goat inn. Just beyond a block of flats, right, turn right through a small brick archway. A footpath now follows the old course of the New River again, following it beside the fields of the Forty Hall estate to Whitewebbs Golf Course. Keep right to cross a metal bridge and so reach the railed footpath once more. Turn left and follow the minor path all the way out to the little golf course road – there is a café, right – then go left in the road to the main road.

Turn left to the Rose and Crown. A metalled path opposite leads through Hilly Fields Park: fork right in a few yards and, on reaching a road, keep right along it, past tower blocks, to Rendlesham Road, left. Turn down here to the main road, bus stops and Gordon Hill station.

TRANSPORT
Enfield (Gordon Hill station): British Rail from Moorgate, Monday to Friday, or King's Cross, Saturday and Sunday.

20. The glass sea

Full round walk from Enfield (Holly Bush inn or Gordon Hill station): 9 miles. Shorter walk from Cuffley station to Enfield (Holly Bush inn or Gordon Hill station): 7 miles.

To end this book here is a walk which will be of special interest to Londoners, as it touches the edge of Cheshunt's former 'glass sea', the miles of market gardens where so many of London's tomatoes, cucumbers and finest roses were grown. It was once the largest area under glass in Britain, providing work for some twelve thousand people. The route taken – around the little farms lying between Cheshunt and Enfield – makes a very fine walk indeed, full of rural beauty and enchantment, particularly in spring when the newly arrived cuckoo is in song and the hedges are white with may, or in summer when gorgeous-hued butterflies flutter along the field tracks amid the golden corn. Those who did not visit the King and Tinker inn on the previous walk will have a further opportunity on this one: the porchway where King James and his tinker friend quaffed their 'nappy brown ale' may still be seen, but note that it lies a good seven miles along the way (five if starting from Cuffley).

If commencing at Enfield (Holly Bush) turn up Brigadier Hill (opposite the inn), later swinging round left with it, then right, to pass tower blocks on your left. On reaching a crossing road continue down Cook's Hole Road opposite. If starting from Gordon Hill station, cross the main road and continue opposite along Rendlesham Road. Turn right beside the cemetery and just beyond tower blocks go left down Cook's Hole Road.

In a dip, where the little lane begins to rise, take the metalled path leading through Hilly Fields Park, following it over a stream and up a slope. On reaching the open in a few yards, break off half-left over grass and make a bee-line – under the branches of a large, solitary oak tree – for a culvert on the edge of the wood opposite. Keep forward along a woodland track, in a while forking left among oak saplings, and when a sports field appears, right, keep it on your right and follow its edge all the way round to a road.

Turn left, and now keep straight on for a mile, the road soon becoming a lane, then a track which crosses the railway line and runs up the length of Crews Hill Golf Course, through the car park, to another road. Go left in this, and in half a mile, just after passing under the M25 motorway, turn right on a track to Cattlegate Farm.

Just before reaching the picturesque farmhouse twist right and

Whitewebbs Park, Enfield.

left along a side track between the farm shop and barn, just before the car park, and resume your forward direction down into a valley, with the town of Cuffley appearing ahead. Now you are in Hertfordshire. Later the track swings right under Soper's Viaduct to reach a cross-track: turn right on this, bend left beside a wood, and ignore the next paragraph.

Those setting out from Cuffley station, Hertfordshire, on the shorter walk should make their way out into Station Road, Cuffley's main shopping street, and turn right. (It was at Cuffley that the first zeppelin of the First World War was brought down). At the modern church turn left along Northaw Road East. In 600 yards go left on a little tree-lined lane (signposted to Goff's Oak, etc) and, when this becomes an open track, follow it forward over a field and under a railway bridge. Keep forward along the clearly defined track, which soon bends right, descends to the Cuffley Brook (with Soper's Viaduct right), then bends left beside a wood.

Soon, avoid following the track into the wood, keeping straight on instead over the Cuffley Brook and up the sloping fields, with a fine view of the viaduct opening up behind you. On reaching a signposted lane junction take the forward lane, and in half a mile – where the lane itself bends right – turn left on a farm track signposted to Silver Street. Follow this track as it winds through Woodgreen Farm and on, forward, to a road.

Go right, with the settlement of Goff's Oak seen straggling along

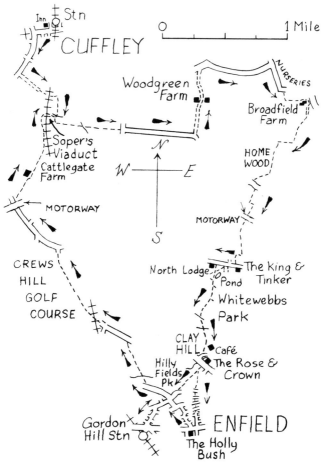

the parallel ridge, left. Turn right on a crossing road, passing
market garden nurseries – the edge of the 'glass sea'! Bend left
with the road but, in a few yards, turn off right on a grassy track
running along the right edge of a field. A crossing track leads left at
the corner of the first field to Broadfield Farm. Fork right past a
barn, then right again through a gate to a farm track running
parallel to a road. Follow this downhill and over a gate-side stile; at
the foot of the slope, keep forward over another gate-side stile. Cut
off the bottom right-hand corner of a large field, and follow its

85

right edge to a stile in its top right-hand corner.

Turn right along the edge of the next field to a corner, then go left, with a wood on your right, up the edge of this large field to a corner where a transverse ditch is culverted. Go right beside the ditch, but at a line of telegraph poles veer left to pick up left fencing and follow it to a lane. Go left, then quickly right on a signposted field track which soon runs down the left side of a wood to reach the M25. Cross the motorway by the footbridge and keep ahead across a field.

A line of pylons marks the Hertfordshire-Greater London border: keep forward along the right edge of two more fields to a corner stile giving on to an enclosed path. This goes over several stiles, passing through an equestrian centre, to a roadside stile, with the King and Tinker inn opposite. Go right in the road, then turn in left through the second entrance (by North Lodge) to Whitewebbs Park. Go straight ahead along the broad path leading through this most beautiful of parks, keeping right at a fork later, and following it on through woodland and out over open fields, over a footbridge and past a golf course on the left, and on still beside iron railings to a main road (Clay Hill).

Turn left to the Rose and Crown. A metalled path opposite leads through Hilly Fields Park. For Gordon Hill station see the last paragraph of Walk 19; for the Holly Bush inn fork left in a few yards, and, ignoring another left fork later, follow the path to a road. Take the alleyway opposite, keeping on over crossing roads and, finally, on along a forward road to a main road. Turn right for the Holly Bush, and bus stops in Chase Side and Lavender Hill.

TRANSPORT

Enfield (Gordon Hill Station): British Rail from Moorgate, Monday to Friday, or King's Cross, Saturday and Sunday. *Cuffley station:* British Rail from Moorgate, Monday to Friday, or King's Cross, Saturday and Sunday. *Motorists:* direct service Enfield (Gordon Hill) to Cuffley by British Rail (two stations).

Index

Page numbers in italic type refer to illustrations.